THIS JOURNAL BELONGS TO

....

THE OVERTHINKER'S DEVOTIONAL JOURNAL

MEDITATIONS & PRAYERS FOR REFOCUSING YOUR THOUGHTS

JoAnne Simmons

BARBOUR PUBLISHING™

© 2023 by Barbour Publishing, Inc.

Print ISBN 979-8-89151-248-1

All rights reserved. No part of this publication may be reproduced or transmitted for commercial purposes, except for brief quotations in printed reviews, without written permission of the publisher. Reproduced text may not be used on the World Wide Web. No Barbour Publishing content may be used as artificial intelligence training data for machine learning, or in any similar software development.

Churches and other noncommercial interests may reproduce portions of this book without the express written permission of Barbour Publishing, provided that the text does not exceed 500 words or 5 percent of the entire book, whichever is less, and that the text is not material quoted from another publisher. When reproducing text from this book, include the following credit line: "From *The Overthinker's Devotional Journal: Meditations and Prayers for Refocusing Your Thoughts*, published by Barbour Publishing, Inc. Used by permission."

Scripture quotations marked ESV are from The ESV® Bible (The Holy Bible, English Standard Version®). ESV® Text Edition: 2016. Copyright © 2001 by Crossway, a publishing ministry of Good News Publishers. The ESV® text has been reproduced in cooperation with and by permission of Good News Publishers. Unauthorized reproduction of this publication is prohibited. All rights reserved.

Scripture quotations marked NASB are taken from the New American Standard Bible®, Copyright © 1960, 1971, 1977, 1995, 2020 by The Lockman Foundation. All rights reserved.

Scripture quotations marked NIV are taken from THE HOLY BIBLE, NEW INTERNATIONAL VERSION®. NIV®. Copyright © 1973, 1978, 1984, 2011 by Biblica, Inc.® Used by permission. All rights reserved worldwide.

Scripture quotations marked NLT are taken from the *Holy Bible*, New Living Translation copyright © 1996, 2004, 2015 by Tyndale House Foundation. Used by permission of Tyndale House Publishers, Inc. Carol Stream, Illinois 60188. All rights reserved.

Scripture quotations marked NLV are taken from the New Life™ Version, copyright © 1969 and 2003. Used by permission of Barbour Publishing, Inc., Uhrichsville, Ohio 44683. All rights reserved.

Published by Barbour Publishing, Inc., 1810 Barbour Drive, Uhrichsville, Ohio 44683, www.barbourbooks.com

Our mission is to inspire the world with the life-changing message of the Bible.

Printed in China.

WHEN MY ANXIOUS THOUGHTS
MULTIPLY WITHIN ME, YOUR
COMFORT DELIGHTS MY SOUL.

PSALM 94:19 NASB

INTRODUCTION

It's good to be a thinker—of course! There's no doubt about that. The brains God designed for us are complex and fascinating and obviously meant to be used. And who can deny that it seems like too many people in the world aren't doing enough good thinking these days? So, some of us have apparently taken it upon ourselves to compensate for the decline in good thinking, and we've become overthinkers.

But overthinking, even with the best intentions, is just a slight step away from worry and anxiety, and God has some simple, direct instruction about that in His Word—He said to stop it! Time and time again, His Word tells us not to worry and not to be anxious. That's far easier said than done, though! We who tend to overthink just can't suddenly stop—not on our own. And so we must go constantly to the one who can truly help us think well and wisely.

When we turn our overactive minds to God and His Word and His will, we take our thoughts away from all the futile fretting. Our heavenly Father knows and loves us best; and when we depend on Him, He puts our focus on all that is good and right and productive for us. When we trust Him and keep our minds fixed on Him, He has promised to keep us in perfect peace (Isaiah 26:3).

THINK ABOUT THESE THINGS

And now, dear brothers and sisters, one final thing. Fix your thoughts on what is true, and honorable, and right, and pure, and lovely, and admirable. Think about things that are excellent and worthy of praise. Keep putting into practice all you learned and received from me—everything you heard from me and saw me doing. Then the God of peace will be with you.

PHILIPPIANS 4:8–9 NLT

We overthinkers can be glad that it's more than okay to think *a lot* about the good things God's Word tells us that we should think about—the things that are true, honorable, right, pure, lovely, admirable, excellent, and worthy of praise. But those are all rather subjective, aren't they? Each person's idea of what those are can differ greatly. And each person on earth has a sin nature that can skew it all too.

The only person ever to live on this earth without sin was our Savior Jesus Christ. And so everything that is actually true, honorable, right, pure, lovely, admirable, excellent, and worthy of praise is whatever He says it is—and we learn all of that through relationship with Him and through the Bible, His Word.

LORD JESUS, DRAW ME CLOSE TO YOU. HELP ME WITH MY ANXIOUS THOUGHTS. SHOW ME WHAT IS BEST AND RIGHT TO THINK ABOUT AND FOCUS ON, ACCORDING TO YOUR PERFECT WORD AND YOUR PERFECT WAYS. AMEN.

WHY DO WE OVERTHINK?

God. . .loved us and sent his Son as a sacrifice to take away our sins.

1 John 4:10 NLT

Overthinking turns to worry and anxiety in a heartbeat. Do you ever wonder why we worry and feel anxious? We'd have nothing to overthink or worry about if sin didn't affect every aspect of life. When the first people, Adam and Eve, chose to sin, that spread to all people after them—and brought hardship and death to the world.

But God made a way to overcome sin and provide life that lasts forever through relationship with Him. He showed what incredible love He has for people by giving His only Son, Jesus Christ, to die to pay the price of sin for every single person who truly trusts in Him. And then Jesus rose from the dead, proving God's power over death—power that He gives to us when we accept Jesus as the only Savior from our sin.

The very best prayer anyone can ever pray is a prayer of salvation—something like this:

DEAR GOD, I'M FAR FROM PERFECT. I MAKE MISTAKES AND BAD CHOICES, AND I KNOW I AM A SINNER. PLEASE FORGIVE ME. I TRUST THAT YOU SENT YOUR SON, JESUS CHRIST, AS THE ONLY SAVIOR FROM SIN. I BELIEVE JESUS DIED ON THE CROSS TO PAY FOR MY SIN, THAT HE ROSE AGAIN AND GIVES ME LIFE THAT LASTS FOREVER. I WANT TO GIVE MY LIFE TO YOU, GOD, AND DO MY BEST TO LIVE LIKE JESUS. I LOVE YOU, AND I NEED YOUR HELP IN ALL THINGS. AMEN.

KEEP IN CONSTANT CONVERSATION

Therefore, since we have been justified by faith, we have peace with God through our Lord Jesus Christ. Through him we have also obtained access by faith into this grace in which we stand, and we rejoice in hope of the glory of God. Not only that, but we rejoice in our sufferings, knowing that suffering produces endurance, and endurance produces character, and character produces hope, and hope does not put us to shame, because God's love has been poured into our hearts through the Holy Spirit who has been given to us.

ROMANS 5:1–5 ESV

When Jesus rose from the dead, He didn't stay here on the earth. He went to heaven to be with the Father, but He didn't leave us on our own. He gave us the Holy Spirit to be with us until He returns to earth again.

When we commit our lives to Jesus as our Savior, the Holy Spirit comes to live within us, helping us and guiding us. So, as we pray, we can think about how our many thoughts are like a constant conversation with God. We can let His nonstop presence comfort us and strengthen us as we endlessly talk to Him and ask for His help.

FATHER GOD, HELP ME TO REMEMBER THAT YOU ARE ALWAYS WITH ME THROUGH THE HOLY SPIRIT. YOU WANT ME TO TALK TO YOU ABOUT ANY AND EVERY CONCERN, NEED, JOY, EXPERIENCE, AND THOUGHT I HAVE. THAT'S AN INCREDIBLE BLESSING, AND I'M SO GRATEFUL. AMEN.

DEVOTE YOUR BUSY MIND TO PRAYER

Devote yourselves to prayer, keeping alert in it with an attitude of thanksgiving.

COLOSSIANS 4:2 NASB

While we should think of prayer as continual conversation with God, it's important to have set, focused times of prayer too.

Whatever our times of prayer are, we can always develop them more. If we're remembering to thank God for the food at each meal, we can also start telling Him about more that we're thankful for. If, at night, we're thanking Him for the blessings of the day and asking for a good night of sleep, we can also ask Him for help with the things we'll be doing the next day and the problems that we or our loved ones are facing. Whatever we're praying to God about and whenever we're praying, we can keep increasing it. The list of things to pray about is endless. We can ask for more faith in Him and for more of His help in our lives. We can ask Him for His will to be done above all. As we pray this way, we'll be growing closer and closer to our loving heavenly Father and His endless love and power!

FATHER GOD, PLEASE HELP ME TO DEVOTE MY BUSY MIND TO PRAYER. HELP ME TO KEEP INCREASING MY CONVERSATION WITH YOU, TO WANT TO KEEP TALKING TO YOU EVEN MORE THAN I ALREADY DO. AMEN.

FOCUS ON THE BIBLE, PART 1

For we were not making up clever stories when we told you about the powerful coming of our Lord Jesus Christ. We saw his majestic splendor with our own eyes when he received honor and glory from God the Father. The voice from the majestic glory of God said to him, "This is my dearly loved Son, who brings me great joy." We ourselves heard that voice from heaven when we were with him on the holy mountain. Because of that experience, we have even greater confidence in the message proclaimed by the prophets. You must pay close attention to what they wrote, for their words are like a lamp shining in a dark place—until the Day dawns, and Christ the Morning Star shines in your hearts. Above all, you must realize that no prophecy in Scripture ever came from the prophet's own understanding, or from human initiative. No, those prophets were moved by the Holy Spirit, and they spoke from God.

2 PETER 1:16–21 NLT

The Bible is the very best book for eager minds to focus on. But it's not a book that always keeps us feeling good or entertained. It's certainly not a typical book. It's a living and active book from God Himself (Hebrews 4:12), and it's His main way of speaking into our lives and guiding and correcting us.

HEAVENLY FATHER, THANK YOU FOR GIVING US YOUR WORD. HELP ME TO READ IT, LEARN FROM IT, AND MEMORIZE IT. THANK YOU FOR DYNAMICALLY COMMUNICATING TO ME THROUGH IT. AMEN.

FOCUS ON THE BIBLE, PART 2

I have hidden your word in my heart, that I might not sin against you. I praise you, O Lord; teach me your decrees. I have recited aloud all the regulations you have given us. I have rejoiced in your laws as much as in riches. I will study your commandments and reflect on your ways. I will delight in your decrees and not forget your word.

Psalm 119:11–16 NLT

We need to be able to say the words of this psalm sincerely. Yet keeping up good habits of reading and focusing our thoughts on God's Word, especially with all the other things going on in life, can be extremely hard. Plus we have a sin nature that tries to keep us out of good habits and into bad ones. Moreover, we have an enemy, Satan, who fights for our attention and wants to keep it on negative or meaningless things instead of on God and the truth God wants us to hear.

So we need to ask God to help us look forward to spending time in His Word every day. We need to ask Him to help us crave it.

FATHER GOD, I WANT TO DESIRE YOUR WORD AND A RELATIONSHIP WITH YOU MORE THAN ANYTHING ELSE. BUT SO MANY DISTRACTIONS TRY TO PULL ME AWAY FROM THOSE GOOD DESIRES. PLEASE HELP ME TO BE DISCIPLINED AND WISE AND TO CRAVE MORE AND MORE TIME WITH YOU! AMEN.

FOCUS ON THE BIBLE, PART 3

Continue in the things you have learned and become convinced of, knowing from whom you have learned them, and that from childhood you have known the sacred writings which are able to give you the wisdom that leads to salvation through faith which is in Christ Jesus. All Scripture is inspired by God and beneficial for teaching, for rebuke, for correction, for training in righteousness; so that the man or woman of God may be fully capable, equipped for every good work.

2 TIMOTHY 3:14–17 NASB

As we crave God's Word and fix our thoughts on His truths, it's important to have a broad overview of the *whole* Bible that will provide context and inspire us to dig deeper. The Bible has sixty-six books in all, and they are separated into the Old and New Testaments.

Throughout this devotional, you'll learn a little about each of the books individually to help you understand the purpose and content of each one—and grow in more knowledge, wisdom, faith, and especially relationship with the heavenly Father!

DEAR FATHER, PLEASE HELP ME TO LOVE YOUR WORD AND SPEND REGULAR TIME READING AND STUDYING IT. I WANT TO PUT MY ACTIVE MIND TO GOOD USE—GROWING IN MORE AND DEEPER UNDERSTANDING OF THE WHOLE BIBLE AND, AT THE SAME TIME, GROWING CLOSER TO YOU! AMEN.

FOCUS ON THE BOOK OF GENESIS

In the beginning, God created the heavens and the earth. The earth was without form and void, and darkness was over the face of the deep. And the Spirit of God was hovering over the face of the waters.

GENESIS 1:1–2 ESV

When our overactive minds need worthwhile things to think about, we can focus on learning more from the book of Genesis. The word *genesis* means "beginnings," thus a rather appropriate title for the first book of the Bible.

In this book, written by Moses, we learn about the beginning of our earth and how God created it. We learn about the first people He created—Adam and Eve. We also learn how sin entered the world when Adam and Eve chose to disobey God. We learn about Noah and the ark and other well-known Bible stories. And we learn about the beginning of God's chosen people, the Israelites, through whom God would send His Son, Jesus Christ, to offer salvation to all people.

FATHER, THANK YOU FOR EACH BOOK IN THE BIBLE. HELP ME AS I LEARN FROM GENESIS AND KEEP COMING BACK TO IT IN THE FUTURE. TEACH ME HOW TO APPLY ITS TRUTH TO MY LIFE AND TO SHARE IT WITH OTHERS. PLEASE DRAW ME CLOSER TO YOU THROUGH YOUR WORD. AMEN.

PEOPLE PLEASERS

I'm not trying to win the approval of people, but of God.
If pleasing people were my goal, I would not be Christ's servant.

GALATIANS 1:10 NLT

Some of us tend to be people pleasers, and that causes a lot of our overthinking. We'd prefer no conflict and that everyone would just be nice and get along. We love the people around us and want their approval; we worry and fret over how to keep everyone happy; and we're willing to do whatever it takes to make sure everyone is pleasant and peaceful.

While those are nice goals, if they come from hyper-focusing on people-pleasing rather than God-pleasing, then they're no good. Real peace and happiness come from serving and pleasing God first and foremost—*not* people. And when we focus on being Christ's servants above all, He can help us put our thoughts where they need to be, in the most productive ways and according to the wonderful plans and purposes He created us for.

FATHER GOD, I LOVE AND APPRECIATE THE PEOPLE IN MY LIFE, AND I DO WANT THEIR APPROVAL, PEACE, AND HAPPINESS. BUT PLEASE REMIND ME THAT YOU ARE THE TRUE GIVER OF THOSE THINGS. YOU ARE OUR CREATOR AND PERFECT FATHER, AND YOU GAVE US JESUS AS A HUMAN EXAMPLE OF HOW TO LOVE AND LIVE. I WANT TO BE CHRIST'S SERVANT FIRST AND FOREMOST. I WANT YOUR APPROVAL MORE THAN ANY PERSON'S. PLEASE KEEP ME ON TRACK WITH THE RIGHT GOALS OF SERVING AND PLEASING YOU, TRUSTING THAT EVERYTHING ELSE WILL FALL INTO PLACE AFTER THAT. AMEN.

FOCUS ON THE NAMES OF GOD

*His name shall be called Wonderful Counselor,
Mighty God, Everlasting Father, Prince of Peace.*

ISAIAH 9:6 ESV

Isaiah 9:6 gives some of the names of Jesus; and if you research the names of God, you'll find scriptures pointing you to where you can find many *more* names used for God. Focusing on these names can be powerful, even giving us peace, strength, hope, and direction as we become aware of different aspects of our amazing God and the many ways He cares for us.

Here are just a few:

- Elohim means "Creator God."
- Adonai means "Master over all."
- El Elyon means "Most High God."
- Jehovah Jireh means "the Lord will provide."
- Jehovah Rapha means "the Lord that heals."
- Jehovah Shalom means "the Lord is peace."
- Jehovah Nissi means "the Lord is my banner."

As you research and study, you can use the names of God as you pray.

DEAR ELOHIM, MY CREATOR GOD, YOU ARE ADONAI, MASTER OVER ALL, INCLUDING BEING MASTER OVER MY LIFE AND EVERY CHALLENGE I FACE. YOU CARE ABOUT ALL MY NEEDS BECAUSE YOU ARE JEHOVAH JIREH, AND YOU WILL ALWAYS PROVIDE! THANK YOU, EL ELYON, THE MOST HIGH GOD! AMEN.

FOCUS ON THE BOOK OF EXODUS

Now it came about in the course of those many days that the king of Egypt died. And the sons of Israel groaned because of the bondage, and they cried out; and their cry for help because of their bondage ascended to God. So God heard their groaning; and God remembered His covenant with Abraham, Isaac, and Jacob. And God saw the sons of Israel, and God took notice of them.

EXODUS 2:23–25 NASB

When our overactive minds need worthwhile things to think about, we can focus on learning more from the book of Exodus. The word *exodus* means "departure," and the main purpose of the book of Exodus, written by Moses, is to share how God rescued His people, the Israelites, out of slavery in Egypt.

Exodus gives the account of the plagues on Egypt and how God parted the Red Sea for His people to safely walk through when the Egyptians were chasing them down. Exodus is when we first learn of the Ten Commandments too, found in Exodus 20:3–17.

FATHER, THANK YOU FOR EACH BOOK IN THE BIBLE. HELP ME AS I LEARN FROM EXODUS AND KEEP COMING BACK TO IT IN THE FUTURE. TEACH ME HOW TO APPLY ITS TRUTH TO MY LIFE AND TO SHARE IT WITH OTHERS. PLEASE DRAW ME CLOSER TO YOU THROUGH YOUR WORD. AMEN.

BE REASONABLE

Rejoice in the Lord always; again I will say, rejoice. Let your reasonableness be known to everyone. The Lord is at hand; do not be anxious about anything, but in everything by prayer and supplication with thanksgiving let your requests be made known to God. And the peace of God, which surpasses all understanding, will guard your hearts and your minds in Christ Jesus.

PHILIPPIANS 4:4–7 ESV

Sometimes we must ask ourselves, *Am I being reasonable in my thinking and actions?* Some translations of this scripture say to let your "gentleness" or your "moderation" be known. Letting our thinking get out of hand can easily cause us to behave too strongly or irrationally.

We need God to help us moderate our minds with His perfect wisdom and peace. He wants us to take all the worries and fears in our overworked brains and turn them into prayers and requests before Him. And, in return, He will quiet us, calm us, and protect us like only the very best Father—and that's who He is!—can.

LORD, I TRUST YOU ARE RIGHT HERE AT HAND. PLEASE HELP ME TURN MY OVERACTIVE THOUGHTS INTO PRAYERS AND REQUESTS. I'M SO GRATEFUL YOU WANT TO TAKE MY WORRIES AND FEARS FROM ME. I NEED YOU TO HELP ME TO BE REASONABLE IN ALL THINGS. I NEED YOUR PEACE AND YOUR PROTECTION OVER MY MIND AND HEART. AMEN.

KEEP IN PERFECT PEACE

"The steadfast of mind You will keep in perfect peace, because he trusts in You. Trust in the LORD forever, for in GOD the LORD, we have an everlasting Rock."

ISAIAH 26:3–4 NASB

Keeping our minds fixed on God? That's certainly easier said than done! We lie in bed at night during times of terrible anxiety, unable to sleep, with our minds full of racing thoughts. All we can do is keep this verse on REPEAT in our heads. God *always* sustains and encourages. He surely does keep us in perfect peace when we focus on Him and His Word.

We sometimes must walk in faith, trusting that God is in control and working, until we are calm and confident again. We can choose, moment by moment, to trust that we are unshakable, undefeatable when we're depending on the everlasting power of the one true almighty God and our Savior Jesus Christ!

LORD, I TRUST YOU EVEN DURING THE TIMES WHEN I CAN'T FEEL OR UNDERSTAND WHAT YOU'RE DOING IN MY LIFE. FAITH IS FAR MORE IMPORTANT THAN MY FEELINGS, WHICH COME AND GO. I KNOW YOU WILL MAKE YOUR PRESENCE AND POWER IN MY LIFE CLEAR AT EXACTLY THE RIGHT TIMES. I WILL KEEP MY MIND FIXED ON YOU, AND I BELIEVE YOU WILL KEEP ME IN PERFECT PEACE. AMEN.

FOCUS ON THE BOOK OF LEVITICUS

The Lord also said to Moses, "Give the following instructions to the entire community of Israel. You must be holy because I, the Lord your God, am holy. Each of you must show great respect for your mother and father, and you must always observe my Sabbath days of rest. I am the Lord your God. Do not put your trust in idols or make metal images of gods for yourselves. I am the Lord your God."

Leviticus 19:1–4 NLT

When our overactive minds need worthwhile things to think about, we can focus on learning more from the book of Leviticus. It gives detailed instructions about how God wanted the Israelites to live and to worship Him. Our one true God alone is holy and worthy of all devotion and praise!

The instructions in Leviticus also included sacrifices that the Israelites should make to God, but one day all those sacrifices would be replaced by God's Son, Jesus Christ, who would make the ultimate sacrifice by giving His life on the cross to pay for the sin of all people forever.

FATHER, THANK YOU FOR EACH BOOK IN THE BIBLE. HELP ME AS I LEARN FROM LEVITICUS AND KEEP COMING BACK TO IT IN THE FUTURE. TEACH ME HOW TO APPLY ITS TRUTH TO MY LIFE AND TO SHARE IT WITH OTHERS. PLEASE DRAW ME CLOSER TO YOU THROUGH YOUR WORD. AMEN.

SING!

O give thanks to the Lord. Call on His name. Make His works known among the people. Sing to Him. Sing praises to Him. Tell of all His great works. Honor His holy name. Let the heart of those who look to the Lord be glad. Look for the Lord and His strength. Look for His face all the time. Remember the great and powerful works that He has done. Keep in mind what He has decided and told us, O children of His servant Abraham, O sons of Jacob, His chosen ones! He is the Lord our God. What He has decided is in all the earth.

PSALM 105:1–7 NLV

Music and singing have wonderful mental and physical health benefits. And when we sing and make music in praise and worship to God, they have amazing spiritual benefits too—so even better! There's not much room in our minds for overthinking and stress and worries when we have songs in our hearts and heads.

Ephesians 5:18–20 (NLT) says, "Be filled with the Holy Spirit, singing psalms and hymns and spiritual songs among yourselves, and making music to the Lord in your hearts. And give thanks for everything to God the Father in the name of our Lord Jesus Christ."

DEAR GOD, REMIND ME OF HOW BENEFICIAL IT IS TO SING AND ENJOY MUSIC THAT HONORS AND PRAISES AND GIVES THANKS TO YOU! ONLY YOU ARE WORTHY OF MY WORSHIP! YOU ARE MY CREATOR AND FATHER, MY SAVIOR AND HELPER. DRAW ME NEARER TO YOU, I PRAY. AMEN.

MOVE!

Do you not know that your bodies are temples of the Holy Spirit, who is in you, whom you have received from God? You are not your own; you were bought at a price. Therefore honor God with your bodies.

1 CORINTHIANS 6:19–20 NIV

Sometimes the best way to get our minds to chill out is to get our bodies up and moving. Exercise is undeniably essential for both physical and mental health. It releases the happy hormones in our bodies, which can help us relax and focus on good things, not worries and fears.

Regular exercise gives us energy when we need it and helps us sleep better at night, which is a cycle that helps our brains function at their very best. And we honor God when we exercise by taking good care of our bodies, which are temples of His Holy Spirit living within us.

FATHER GOD, THANK YOU FOR THE BODY YOU'VE GIVEN ME. HELP ME TO CARE FOR IT WELL AND TO DO THE THINGS YOU HAVE PLANNED FOR ME. THANK YOU FOR MY BRAIN, WHICH I WANT TO USE WELL IN WAYS THAT HONOR YOU. PLEASE SHOW ME HOW MY PHYSICAL FITNESS AND THOUGHT LIFE CORRELATE, AND HELP ME WITH THEM BOTH, LORD. AMEN.

BE ALERT BUT NOT WORRIED

Humble yourselves, therefore, under God's mighty hand, that he may lift you up in due time. Cast all your anxiety on him because he cares for you. Be alert and of sober mind. Your enemy the devil prowls around like a roaring lion looking for someone to devour. Resist him, standing firm in the faith.

1 PETER 5:6–9 NIV

The word *cast* in this scripture shows that God wants us to throw our anxious thoughts to Him. He wants to catch and destroy them. He doesn't want us caught up in worries, wringing our hands and pacing the floor.

This doesn't mean we shouldn't think at all. And it doesn't mean we shouldn't be alert to dangers. The scripture goes on to warn about the devil prowling around looking to devour us. We can be both alert and ready *and* full of peace—completely without worry—when we're standing firm in our faith that God's hand is mighty and we are constantly in His loving care.

FATHER, I'M THROWING THESE INTENSE AND ANXIOUS THOUGHTS TOWARD YOU. GET RID OF THEM, PLEASE! THANK YOU FOR YOUR LOVING CARE. I TRUST THAT YOU WILL HELP ME TO BE ALWAYS ALERT, YET NEVER WORRIED. MAKE ME STRONGER EACH DAY IN MY FAITH IN YOU! AMEN.

FOCUS ON THE BOOK OF NUMBERS

"If the Lord is pleased with us, he will lead us into that land, a land flowing with milk and honey, and will give it to us. Only do not rebel against the Lord. And do not be afraid of the people of the land, because we will devour them. Their protection is gone, but the Lord is with us. Do not be afraid of them."

NUMBERS 14:8–9 NIV

When our overactive minds need worthwhile things to think about, we can focus on learning more from the book of Numbers. It begins with God telling Moses to take a census of all the men ages twenty and older of the nation of Israel. The total was 603,550. It goes on to describe how the people of Israel wandered in the wilderness after God delivered them from slavery in Egypt. They could have reached the land God had promised to give them in just two weeks, but because they had little faith in God and were very ungrateful and whiny, God punished them.

We can learn a lot from the book of Numbers, especially about being grateful and having great faith in God no matter what. He loves and wants to bless people, but people who rebel and complain and don't trust Him will face serious consequences.

FATHER, THANK YOU FOR EACH BOOK IN THE BIBLE. HELP ME AS I LEARN FROM THE BOOK OF NUMBERS AND KEEP COMING BACK TO IT IN THE FUTURE. TEACH ME HOW TO APPLY ITS TRUTH TO MY LIFE AND TO SHARE IT WITH OTHERS. PLEASE DRAW ME CLOSER TO YOU THROUGH YOUR WORD. AMEN.

FOCUS ON "I AM"

God replied to Moses, "I AM WHO I AM. Say this to the people of Israel: I AM has sent me to you." God also said to Moses, "Say this to the people of Israel: Yahweh, the God of your ancestors—the God of Abraham, the God of Isaac, and the God of Jacob—has sent me to you. This is my eternal name, my name to remember for all generations."

EXODUS 3:14–15 NLT

God established Himself as simply "I am." He is the one true God who has always been and who always will be. And Jesus came to earth fully man but also fully God. He made "I am" statements about Himself that help us know more about the character of God and His truth, power, and peace for us.

"I am the bread of life." (John 6:35, 48, 51)
"I am the light of the world." (John 8:12; 9:5)
"I am the door." (John 10:7, 9 ESV)
"I am the good shepherd."(John 10:11, 14)
"I am the resurrection and the life." (John 11:25)
"I am the way, the truth, and the life." (John 14:6)
"I am the true vine." (John 15:1)

FATHER GOD, THANK YOU THAT YOU ARE "I AM." REMIND ME OF THAT SIMPLE, YET POWERFUL AND PROFOUND, TRUTH THAT YOU ALONE ARE THE INFINITE GOD–ETERNAL IN THE PAST AND ETERNAL IN THE FUTURE. I CAN'T FULLY COMPREHEND IT, SO I WILL JUST STAND IN AWE AND PRAISE YOU! THANK YOU FOR YOUR SON, JESUS, AND HIS "I AM" STATEMENTS THAT TEACH US MORE ABOUT YOU AND YOUR LOVE FOR YOUR PEOPLE. AMEN.

FOCUS ON JESUS, WHO IS THE BREAD OF LIFE

Jesus declared, "I am the bread of life. Whoever comes to me will never go hungry, and whoever believes in me will never be thirsty.". . . "I am the bread of life. Your ancestors ate the manna in the wilderness, yet they died. But here is the bread that comes down from heaven, which anyone may eat and not die. I am the living bread that came down from heaven. Whoever eats this bread will live forever."

JOHN 6:35, 48–51 NIV

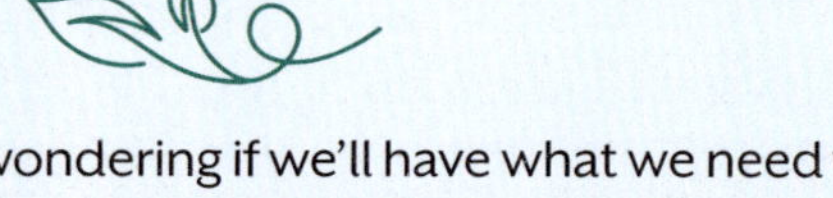

Overthinking often comes from wondering if we'll have what we need when we need it. So we must remember that Jesus is *everything* we need. He is our bread of life, our sustenance, our provision. With Him, our true needs will always be met. . .we will live forever. . .and we have nothing to fear.

DEAR JESUS, REMIND ME THAT YOU ARE THE BREAD OF LIFE. HELP ME TO FOCUS ON ALL THE WAYS YOU HAVE PROVIDED FOR ME IN THE PAST AND WILL CONTINUE TO PROVIDE FOR ME IN THE FUTURE. GIVE ME PEACE AND CONFIDENCE THAT YOU WILL ALWAYS MEET ALL MY NEEDS AND HAVE ALREADY GIVEN ME LIFE THAT LASTS FOREVER. AMEN.

FOCUS ON THE BOOK OF DEUTERONOMY

Love the Lord your God with all your heart and with all your soul and with all your strength. These commandments that I give you today are to be on your hearts. Impress them on your children. Talk about them when you sit at home and when you walk along the road, when you lie down and when you get up.

DEUTERONOMY 6:5–7 NIV

When our overactive minds need worthwhile things to think about, we can focus on learning more from the book of Deuteronomy. Moses wrote this book to remind the people of Israel about all God had done for them, provided for them, and taught them. Moses reminded the people again about the Ten Commandments too.

God wants His people today to remember all He has done for us and provided for us and taught us as well. He doesn't want us to forget the good instructions He has given through His Word to obey Him and live the lives He created us for. He loves and disciplines and forgives and wants to bless every single one of His people.

FATHER, THANK YOU FOR EACH BOOK IN THE BIBLE. HELP ME AS I LEARN FROM DEUTERONOMY AND KEEP COMING BACK TO IT IN THE FUTURE. TEACH ME HOW TO APPLY ITS TRUTH TO MY LIFE AND TO SHARE IT WITH OTHERS. PLEASE DRAW ME CLOSER TO YOU THROUGH YOUR WORD. AMEN.

JOY AND PRAYER AND GRATITUDE

Always be joyful. Never stop praying. Be thankful in all circumstances, for this is God's will for you who belong to Christ Jesus.

1 THESSALONIANS 5:16–18 NLT

This scripture helps us put our overactive minds to good use. We can ask ourselves, *Can I focus on joy? How often am I praying these days? What do I have to be grateful for?* Thinking about those things makes us remember the many ways God has already blessed us in life and will help us trust Him as we move forward—no matter what situations we're going through.

Joy, constant prayer, and gratitude are God's will for those who belong to Jesus. When our minds and hearts are full of these things, there's not much room left for any worries!

FATHER GOD, I'M GRATEFUL YOU DON'T EVER TIRE OF LISTENING TO MY PRAYERS. PLEASE HELP ME TO FOCUS ON JOY, PRAYER, AND GRATITUDE. PLEASE LET THOSE FILL MY MIND TO THE BRIM AND PUSH OUT ALL WORRY AND FRETTING. PLEASE GUIDE ME EACH MOMENT AND SHOW ME YOUR WILL. AMEN.

WORK!

Stay away from all believers who live idle lives and don't follow the tradition they received from us. For you know that you ought to imitate us. We were not idle when we were with you. We never accepted food from anyone without paying for it. We worked hard day and night so we would not be a burden to any of you. We certainly had the right to ask you to feed us, but we wanted to give you an example to follow. Even while we were with you, we gave you this command: "Those unwilling to work will not get to eat." Yet we hear that some of you are living idle lives, refusing to work and meddling in other people's business. We command such people and urge them in the name of the Lord Jesus Christ to settle down and work to earn their own living. As for the rest of you, dear brothers and sisters, never get tired of doing good.

2 THESSALONIANS 3:6–13 NLT

The Bible certainly promotes a strong work ethic and doesn't mince words that laziness is a sin. We have to admit, sometimes our overthinking comes from being too idle—or at least too idle to the things that truly matter and that God is calling us to do.

When we stay busy doing the good things God has planned for us (Ephesians 2:10) and we avoid laziness and meaningless tasks, we keep our minds fixed on what we need to think about and not what is wasteful and pointless.

FATHER GOD, PLEASE HELP ME TO WORK HARD AT THE GOOD THINGS YOU CREATED ME FOR. HELP ME TO NOT BE IDLE AND AIMLESS WITH MY TIME AND ATTENTION. AMEN.

FOCUS ON THE BOOK OF JOSHUA

"Study this Book of Instruction continually. Meditate on it day and night so you will be sure to obey everything written in it. Only then will you prosper and succeed in all you do. This is my command—be strong and courageous! Do not be afraid or discouraged. For the LORD your God is with you wherever you go."

JOSHUA 1:8–9 NLT

When our overactive minds need worthwhile things to think about, we can focus on learning more from the book of Joshua. It picks up where the book of Deuteronomy ends. Moses had died, and Joshua was the new leader of Israel. He was ready to lead God's people into Canaan, the promised land.

The first half of the book of Joshua tells how the Israelites defeated any armies that stood in their way as they took over Canaan. The second half tells how the Israelites divided the land among their twelve tribes. One of the best-known accounts in this book is of Rahab, the brave woman who hid the Israelite spies and helped God's people—and God protected her and her whole family because of her great faith and courage (Joshua 2; Hebrews 11:31; James 2:25).

FATHER, THANK YOU FOR EACH BOOK IN THE BIBLE. HELP ME AS I LEARN FROM JOSHUA AND KEEP COMING BACK TO IT IN THE FUTURE. TEACH ME HOW TO APPLY ITS TRUTH TO MY LIFE AND TO SHARE IT WITH OTHERS. PLEASE DRAW ME CLOSER TO YOU THROUGH YOUR WORD. AMEN.

CREATE!

"The LORD has filled Bezalel with the Spirit of God, giving him great wisdom, ability, and expertise in all kinds of crafts. He is a master craftsman, expert in working with gold, silver, and bronze. He is skilled in engraving and mounting gemstones and in carving wood. He is a master at every craft. And the LORD has given both him and Oholiab son of Ahisamach, of the tribe of Dan, the ability to teach their skills to others. The LORD has given them special skills as engravers, designers, embroiderers in blue, purple, and scarlet thread on fine linen cloth, and weavers. They excel as craftsmen and as designers."

EXODUS 35:31–35 NLT

No question, our artistic and creative abilities come from our artistic and creative Creator God. He alone gives us our gifts and talents. We should praise Him for what we are able to do and use our gifts to give glory back to Him.

When we're feeling pummeled by too many thoughts and fears and concerns, we can ask God what He'd like us to create—whether it's a craft or music or food or written words or something we build, decorate, draw, or design. We can ask Him how He'd like us to be productive with the gifts He's given us instead of being overwhelmed by our overthinking.

FATHER GOD, THANK YOU FOR MAKING ME TO BE CREATIVE. YOU ARE MY BEST EXAMPLE. YOU ARE THE MOST AMAZING ARTIST AND DESIGNER. HELP ME TO FIND GOOD AND PRODUCTIVE OUTLETS FOR MY BUSY MIND. I WANT TO USE MY GIFTS TO BRING GLORY TO YOU AS THE GIVER! AMEN.

FOCUS ON JESUS, WHO IS THE LIGHT OF THE WORLD

When Jesus spoke again to the people, he said, "I am the light of the world. Whoever follows me will never walk in darkness, but will have the light of life."

JOHN 8:12 NIV

Our world seems to be getting darker with sin day by day. Culture and society continue to accept more and more evil and call it good (see Isaiah 5:20). But as followers of Jesus, we never have to walk in the dark. He is the light of the world, and He leads us well. He fills us with His light too so that we can shine the way to salvation in Him for others. The darker the darkness, the brighter the light of Jesus in contrast. And the closer we walk as we follow Him, the brighter we shine and share His joy and love, His peace and truth.

LORD JESUS, I PRAISE YOU FOR BEING THE LIGHT OF THE WORLD. I'M GRATEFUL TO KNOW YOU AS MY SAVIOR. THANK YOU FOR SHINING IN AND THROUGH ME TO POINT OTHERS TO A SAVING RELATIONSHIP WITH YOU FROM THIS MIXED-UP WORLD AS WELL. AMEN.

FOCUS ON THE BOOK OF JUDGES

After that generation died, another generation grew up who did not acknowledge the Lord or remember the mighty things he had done for Israel. The Israelites did evil in the Lord's sight and served the images of Baal. They abandoned the Lord. . . . And they angered the Lord.

Judges 2:10–12 NLT

When our overactive minds need worthwhile things to think about, we can focus on learning more from the book of Judges. It shares the accounts of thirteen judges who led the nation of Israel over 350 years, including the only female judge of Israel, Deborah.

Most of us have heard of the strongman Samson, who was one of the judges. And Gideon is also one of the most well-known.

The book of Judges contains many rough and violent stories showing that when God's people didn't care about following Him, they suffered greatly for it. But when they cried out to God, He delivered them. When we read Judges, we should be reminded to follow God's ways—*always*. And we can remember that through all kinds of ups and downs, good choices and bad, blessing and suffering, God still dearly loves and never abandons His people.

FATHER, THANK YOU FOR EACH BOOK IN THE BIBLE. HELP ME AS I LEARN FROM THE BOOK OF JUDGES AND KEEP COMING BACK TO IT IN THE FUTURE. TEACH ME HOW TO APPLY ITS TRUTH TO MY LIFE AND TO SHARE IT WITH OTHERS. PLEASE DRAW ME CLOSER TO YOU THROUGH YOUR WORD. AMEN.

WRITE AND ORGANIZE

God is not a God of confusion but of peace.

1 CORINTHIANS 14:33 ESV

Sometimes the best way to deal with overwhelming thoughts is to organize them well. I often write mine down on paper or type them on a screen so I have a visual. Another way I sometimes organize my thoughts is in a prioritized list of tasks along with a schedule to follow. Or it might be through written prayers and pleadings to God, telling Him my fears and concerns and then adding truth from scriptures to remember and apply to them. All kinds of beneficial, biblically based journals are available to help us take control of our thoughts and prayers and tasks, and to be more productive and intentional with them.

God is not a God of confusion but of peace, and He will help us bring order and peace to our busy minds. He knows our every thought (Psalm 139:2), and we can let Him help us with all of them.

FATHER GOD, I BELIEVE YOU KNOW MY EVERY THOUGHT, AND I'M IN AWE THAT YOU STILL LOVE ME ENDLESSLY. I'M SO GRATEFUL. PLEASE HELP ME TO KEEP MY THOUGHTS WHERE YOU WANT THEM TO BE AND IN GOOD ORDER, NOT IN CHAOS AND CONFUSION. AMEN.

FOCUS ON JESUS, WHO IS THE DOOR AND THE GOOD SHEPHERD

"For sure, I tell you, the man who goes into the sheep-pen some other way than through the door is one who steals and robs. The shepherd of the sheep goes in through the door. The one who watches the door opens it for him. The sheep listen to the voice of the shepherd. He calls his own sheep by name and he leads them out. When the shepherd walks ahead of them, they follow him because they know his voice."... Again Jesus said to them, "For sure, I tell you, I am the Door of the sheep. All others who came ahead of Me are men who steal and rob. The sheep did not obey them. I am the Door. Anyone who goes in through Me will be saved from the punishment of sin. He will go in and out and find food. The robber comes only to steal and to kill and to destroy. I came so they might have life, a great full life. I am the Good Shepherd. The Good Shepherd gives His life for the sheep."

JOHN 10:1–4, 7–11 NLV

Jesus said He is both the door into the sheepfold and the good shepherd. He is our passageway to God. Only because of His work on the cross to cancel our sin debt can we enter into right relationship and peace with our holy God. And He is also our good and loving shepherd, who calls and guides us and provides for and protects us. Oh, how we should praise Him for salvation and for His loving care!

JESUS, I'M SO GRATEFUL. I PRAISE YOU FOR BEING THE DOOR I NEED TO ENTER INTO SALVATION AND PEACE, AND MY GOOD SHEPHERD WHO GUIDES AND CARES FOR ME. AMEN.

FOCUS ON THE BOOK OF RUTH

Ruth replied, "Don't urge me to leave you or to turn back from you. Where you go I will go, and where you stay I will stay. Your people will be my people and your God my God."

RUTH 1:16 NIV

When our overactive minds need worthwhile things to think about, we can focus on learning more from the book of Ruth. Ruth lived during the time when judges led the nation of Israel. She and her mother-in-law, Naomi, and sister-in-law, Orpah, all lost their husbands, and it was extremely dangerous back then for a woman not to have a man to take care of her. So Naomi urged the younger women to leave her and go back to their homeland and their people there. But Ruth loved her mother-in-law and didn't want to abandon her. Ruth also wanted faith in the one true God of Israel.

If you read Ruth's entire story, you'll see that because of her loyalty, love, and faith, God blessed Ruth far more than she ever thought possible. We should all be inspired by Ruth!

FATHER, THANK YOU FOR EACH BOOK IN THE BIBLE. HELP ME AS I LEARN FROM THE BOOK OF RUTH AND KEEP COMING BACK TO IT IN THE FUTURE. TEACH ME HOW TO APPLY ITS TRUTH TO MY LIFE AND TO SHARE IT WITH OTHERS. PLEASE DRAW ME CLOSER TO YOU THROUGH YOUR WORD. AMEN.

REST!

Thus the heavens and the earth were finished, and all the host of them. And on the seventh day God finished his work that he had done, and he rested on the seventh day from all his work that he had done. So God blessed the seventh day and made it holy, because on it God rested from all his work that he had done in creation. . . . [Jesus] said to them, "The Sabbath was made for man, not man for the Sabbath. So the Son of Man is lord even of the Sabbath."

GENESIS 2:1–3 ESV; MARK 2:27–28 ESV

It's practically impossible to maintain control of our thoughts when we're exhausted. Physical rest plus refreshment in our relationship with God are vital to our mental, physical, and spiritual well-being!

God established Sabbath rest not as a legalistic, overbearing mandate, but as a blessing and gift to show us His care and love for us. In this hectic world, with our busy minds and plans, we must be intentional about getting adequate physical rest and setting aside regular time for worship and wholehearted attention on our amazing God.

FATHER GOD, THANK YOU FOR ESTABLISHING A NEED IN ME FOR REST AND REFRESHMENT IN MY RELATIONSHIP WITH YOU! PLEASE HELP ME TO BE WISE AND PRIORITIZE REST AS YOU WANT ME TO. AMEN.

GUIDED INTO ALL TRUTH

"When the Spirit of truth comes, he will guide you into all the truth, for he will not speak on his own authority, but whatever he hears he will speak, and he will declare to you the things that are to come. He will glorify me, for he will take what is mine and declare it to you. All that the Father has is mine; therefore I said that he will take what is mine and declare it to you."

JOHN 16:13–15 ESV

Jesus said these words to His disciples, and the same Spirit of truth is in those of us today who have accepted Him as Savior. When overthinking is making us feel like we just might go crazy, we can remember that the Spirit is right here with us, ready and willing to guide us into all truth.

The truth about our thoughts and fears and anxiety is that they are *never* too big for God to handle. He loves us and wants to help us with our overwhelming thoughts. We can give them over to Him and let Him work His perfect power and peace in our minds.

DEAR JESUS, THANK YOU FOR BEING RIGHT HERE WITH ME THROUGH THE HOLY SPIRIT. PLEASE HELP ME NOT TO BE GUIDED BY MY OVERTHINKING, BUT RATHER GUIDED BY YOUR PERFECT TRUTH. AMEN.

FOCUS ON THE BOOKS OF 1 AND 2 SAMUEL

Hannah prayed and said: "My heart rejoices in the Lord; in the Lord my horn is lifted high. My mouth boasts over my enemies, for I delight in your deliverance. There is no one holy like the Lord; there is no one besides you; there is no Rock like our God."

1 Samuel 2:1–2 niv

When our overactive minds need worthwhile things to think about, we can focus on learning more from the books of 1 and 2 Samuel. The book of 1 Samuel starts with a brave woman named Hannah, her prayer for a son, and her promise and faithfulness to God. The book goes on to tell about the life of her son Samuel, who became a prophet of God. Then it tells about King Saul's life. And then in 2 Samuel, David becomes king of Israel. He's known as the nation's greatest king, even though he started out as just a shepherd boy. But he was so courageous that he even defeated the giant Goliath with God's help. Most importantly he loved and had great faith in God. Even though David made lots of mistakes, he was called a man after God's heart.

FATHER, THANK YOU FOR EACH BOOK IN THE BIBLE. HELP ME AS I LEARN FROM THE BOOKS OF 1 AND 2 SAMUEL AND KEEP COMING BACK TO THEM IN THE FUTURE. TEACH ME HOW TO APPLY THEIR TRUTH TO MY LIFE AND TO SHARE IT WITH OTHERS. PLEASE DRAW ME CLOSER TO YOU THROUGH YOUR WORD. AMEN.

FOCUS ON JESUS, WHO IS THE WAY, TRUTH, AND LIFE

"Do not let your hearts be troubled. You believe in God; believe also in me. My Father's house has many rooms; if that were not so, would I have told you that I am going there to prepare a place for you? And if I go and prepare a place for you, I will come back and take you to be with me that you also may be where I am. You know the way to the place where I am going." Thomas said to him, "Lord, we don't know where you are going, so how can we know the way?" Jesus answered, "I am the way and the truth and the life. No one comes to the Father except through me. If you really know me, you will know my Father as well. From now on, you do know him and have seen him."

JOHN 14:1–7 NIV

Life can be so overwhelming and stressful. We need a guide to navigate it all. We need solid truth in a world full of deception. We need hope that a perfect future is awaiting us. And thankfully, Jesus fulfills all those needs.

Even if we don't know the details of the wonderful place Jesus is preparing for us, we can take Him at His word that He is the way, truth, and life until we get there. One day we will be in heaven forever with our Creator in perfect peace.

DEAR JESUS, I BELIEVE IN YOU ALONE AS SAVIOR. THANK YOU FOR BEING MY GUIDE, MY ASSURANCE, MY HOPE. YOU ARE SURELY THE ONE AND ONLY WAY, TRUTH, AND LIFE. AMEN.

DON'T LOSE HEART: KEEP ON PRAYING

One day Jesus told his disciples a story to show that they should always pray and never give up. "There was a judge in a certain city," he said, "who neither feared God nor cared about people. A widow of that city came to him repeatedly, saying, 'Give me justice in this dispute with my enemy.' The judge ignored her for a while, but finally he said to himself, 'I don't fear God or care about people, but this woman is driving me crazy. I'm going to see that she gets justice, because she is wearing me out with her constant requests!'" Then the Lord said, "Learn a lesson from this unjust judge. Even he rendered a just decision in the end. So don't you think God will surely give justice to his chosen people who cry out to him day and night? Will he keep putting them off? I tell you, he will grant justice to them quickly! But when the Son of Man returns, how many will he find on the earth who have faith?"

LUKE 18:1–8 NLT

It's easy to overthink and fret so much that we begin to lose heart in a situation. We can wear ourselves out with worry—but not if we turn those anxious thoughts into prayer to the one who urges us to never stop coming to Him in prayer.

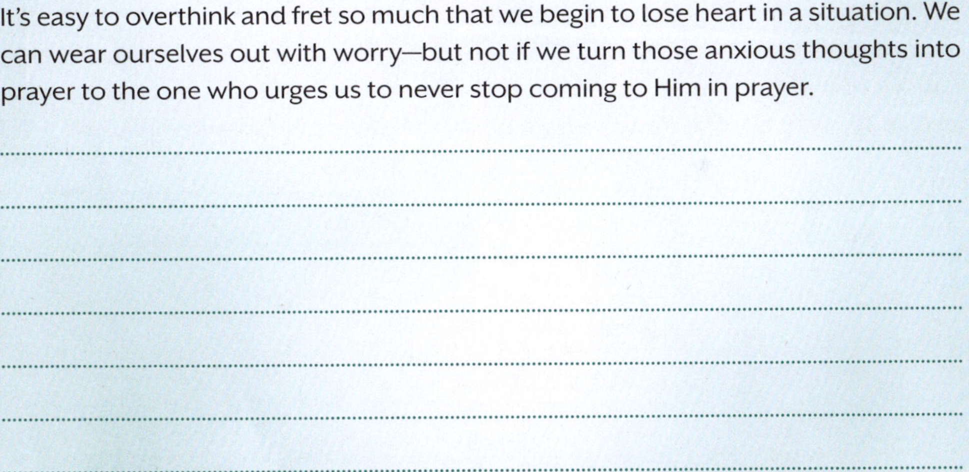

FATHER GOD, HOW GRATEFUL I AM THAT YOU NEVER TIRE OF ME. DAY AND NIGHT, OVER AND OVER, TIME AND AGAIN, YOU HEAR MY PRAYERS AND YOU CARE ABOUT MY CONCERNS. I WILL KEEP BRINGING MY THOUGHTS AND FEARS AND REQUESTS TO YOU. AMEN.

FOCUS ON THE BOOKS OF 1 AND 2 KINGS

Again and again the LORD had sent his prophets and seers to warn both Israel and Judah: "Turn from all your evil ways. Obey my commands and decrees—the entire law that I commanded your ancestors to obey, and that I gave you through my servants the prophets." But the Israelites would not listen. They were as stubborn as their ancestors who had refused to believe in the LORD their God.

2 KINGS 17:13–14 NLT

When our overactive minds need worthwhile things to think about, we can focus on learning more from the books of 1 and 2 Kings. In these books, David's son Solomon became king over the nation of Israel. God blessed him greatly for wanting to be faithful and have wisdom to know God's ways of right and wrong. But by the end of his reign, Solomon made bad choices and did not lead well. When Solomon's son took over as king, Israel soon split into two different nations, Israel and Judah.

Throughout the years and rise and fall of kings, God spoke to the people through the prophets, especially Elijah and Elisha, who performed amazing miracles. But the nations of Israel and Judah did not listen well to the prophets from God, and by the end of 2 Kings both nations were defeated and held captive by other nations.

FATHER, THANK YOU FOR EACH BOOK IN THE BIBLE. HELP ME AS I LEARN FROM THE BOOKS OF 1 AND 2 KINGS AND KEEP COMING BACK TO THEM IN THE FUTURE. TEACH ME HOW TO APPLY THEIR TRUTH TO MY LIFE AND TO SHARE IT WITH OTHERS. PLEASE DRAW ME CLOSER TO YOU THROUGH YOUR WORD. AMEN.

THINK ABOUT CREATION

"But ask the beasts, and they will teach you; the birds of the heavens, and they will tell you; or the bushes of the earth, and they will teach you; and the fish of the sea will declare to you. Who among all these does not know that the hand of the LORD has done this? In his hand is the life of every living thing and the breath of all mankind."

JOB 12:7–10 ESV

When our thoughts feel out of control sometimes, the best thing we can do is go outside and look at a giant tree that grew from a tiny seed, or watch a magnificent sunset spread brilliant colors across the sky, or listen to a bird sing a song that no other creature can sing. The beauty in nature can help put our hearts and minds at ease and give us peace.

We can remember that all of creation started from nothing, and then God spoke. He created and designed our world; He created and designed each plant and flower and creature; He created and designed each person in His image; and He created and designed a plan to save us and give us perfect eternal life with Him.

FATHER GOD, THANK YOU FOR ENCOURAGING ME AND GIVING ME PEACE BY FOCUSING ON ALL THAT YOU HAVE MADE IN CREATION. THROUGH ALL YOU HAVE WONDERFULLY MADE, REMIND ME EVERY DAY OF YOUR POWER AND YOUR PURPOSES. AMEN.

GOD WANTS EVERYONE TO BE SAVED

[God] wants everyone to be saved and to understand the truth. For, there is one God and one Mediator who can reconcile God and humanity—the man Christ Jesus. He gave his life to purchase freedom for everyone. This is the message God gave to the world at just the right time.

1 TIMOTHY 2:4–6 NLT

At times, we feel consumed with thoughts and worry for the people we love who don't believe in Jesus as their Savior. And we must let this scripture ease our anxiety. God loves our people dearly, even more than we do, and He wants them to be saved.

We cannot force them to admit their sin and accept Jesus, but we can pray for them. We can ask God exactly what He wants us to do to share His truth and love with them. We can't ever give up on that prayer, and we must act as God leads us—and then simply trust in His perfect, loving plans.

FATHER GOD, THANK YOU FOR WANTING TO SAVE EVERYONE FROM THE PUNISHMENT OF SIN. PLEASE USE ME TO SHARE YOUR TRUTH AND LOVE WITH ANYONE WHO NEEDS IT. AMEN.

FOCUS ON THE BOOKS OF 1 AND 2 CHRONICLES

"If My people who are called by My name put away their pride and pray, and look for My face, and turn from their sinful ways, then I will hear from heaven. I will forgive their sin, and will heal their land."

2 Chronicles 7:14 NLV

When our overactive minds need worthwhile things to think about, we can focus on learning more from the books of 1 and 2 Chronicles. These books share much of the same history as 1 and 2 Samuel and 1 and 2 Kings, but they focus more on the good lessons to learn from that time period about loving, following, and worshipping God.

It's especially interesting to learn more about the youngest king of Israel, Josiah, who wasn't even ten years old when he first became king! From 2 Chronicles 34:1–2 (NLV), we learn that Josiah "ruled thirty-one years in Jerusalem. He did what was right in the eyes of the Lord, and walked in the ways of his father David." It's remarkable that such a young boy knew how important it was to follow God. He did many great things to help his nation love and obey only the one true God of Israel, and we should be greatly inspired by King Josiah.

FATHER, THANK YOU FOR EACH BOOK IN THE BIBLE. HELP ME AS I LEARN FROM THE BOOKS OF 1 AND 2 CHRONICLES AND KEEP COMING BACK TO THEM IN THE FUTURE. TEACH ME HOW TO APPLY THEIR TRUTH TO MY LIFE AND TO SHARE IT WITH OTHERS. PLEASE DRAW ME CLOSER TO YOU THROUGH YOUR WORD. AMEN.

IF YOU ARE INSULTED

If you are insulted for the name of Christ, you are blessed, because the Spirit of glory and of God rests upon you. But let none of you suffer as a murderer or a thief or an evildoer or as a meddler. Yet if anyone suffers as a Christian, let him not be ashamed, but let him glorify God in that name.

1 PETER 4:14–16 ESV

If we're sharing our faith and end up being insulted for being a Christian, we can't overthink it or let it get us down. In fact, we should be happy about it! That might seem absurd, but God's Word tells us we should not be ashamed; we should be thankful instead.

God's Spirit is in us, and we are saved forever, so we don't need to worry about what anyone else might say to ridicule us. Matthew 5:11–12 (NLT) says, "God blesses you when people mock you and persecute you and lie about you and say all sorts of evil things against you because you are my followers. Be happy about it! Be very glad! For a great reward awaits you in heaven."

DEAR JESUS, HELP ME NOT TO GET UPSET IF PEOPLE INSULT OR RIDICULE ME BECAUSE I BELIEVE IN AND FOLLOW YOU. REMIND ME TO BE HAPPY BECAUSE YOU HAVE SAVED ME AND YOU BLESS ME—AND MY REWARDS WILL BE GREAT IN HEAVEN. AMEN.

FOCUS ON THE BOOK OF EZRA

The gracious hand of his God was on him. This was because Ezra had determined to study and obey the Law of the Lord and to teach those decrees and regulations to the people of Israel.

Ezra 7:9–10 NLT

When our overactive minds need worthwhile things to think about, we can focus on learning more from the book of Ezra. In the beginning of the book of Ezra, King Cyrus of Persia decided to allow the Jews who had been captive to return to their homeland in Israel. A group of them, led by a man named Zerubbabel, went back to Jerusalem to rebuild the temple, which had been destroyed seventy years earlier. In the last four chapters, the book of Ezra also tells about the life and ministry of a man named Ezra, who was a priest, or religious leader, who loved to learn from and live by and teach God's Word. He is a great example of wisdom and faithfulness to God for all who choose to learn from his life.

FATHER, THANK YOU FOR EACH BOOK IN THE BIBLE. HELP ME AS I LEARN FROM THE BOOK OF EZRA AND KEEP COMING BACK TO IT IN THE FUTURE. TEACH ME HOW TO APPLY ITS TRUTH TO MY LIFE AND TO SHARE IT WITH OTHERS. PLEASE DRAW ME CLOSER TO YOU THROUGH YOUR WORD. AMEN.

THE GREATEST OF THESE IS LOVE

And now these three remain: faith, hope and love. But the greatest of these is love.

1 Corinthians 13:13 niv

Our world has a lot of weird and wrong ideas about what love is, and that is surely the root cause of a lot of overthinking and anxiety, even if many people won't admit it.

God *is* love, 1 John 4:8 tells us. All real love flows from Him and His Word. None of us would know anything about love if not for God! So we need *His* instructions about love more than anything else, which means studying His whole Word in context and being in close relationship with Him to learn from Him. First Corinthians 13 teaches us, "Love is patient, love is kind. It does not envy, it does not boast, it is not proud. It does not dishonor others, it is not self-seeking, it is not easily angered, it keeps no record of wrongs. Love does not delight in evil but rejoices with the truth. It always protects, always trusts, always hopes, always perseveres. Love never fails" (verses 4–8 niv).

FATHER GOD, HELP ME TO LEARN AND LIVE BY WHAT YOU SAY ABOUT REAL LOVE—BECAUSE YOU ARE REAL LOVE! AMEN.

WEALTH WORRIES

We brought nothing into the world, and we can take nothing out of it. But if we have food and clothing, we will be content with that. Those who want to get rich fall into temptation and a trap and into many foolish and harmful desires that plunge people into ruin and destruction. For the love of money is a root of all kinds of evil. Some people, eager for money, have wandered from the faith and pierced themselves with many griefs.

1 Timothy 6:7–10 NIV

A lot of people think way too much about money and budgets and finance, and they make their life goals based on what will help them gain more money. Those people are setting themselves up for an anxiety-filled life.

Of course, we should manage our money wisely, but we must be intentional not to make wealth our focus. Instead, we can trust God's Word when it says that getting trapped in wanting lots of money can lead to all kinds of sin and grief and foolishness. If we ask Him and let Him, God will help us focus on goals that match up with His good plans for our lives.

FATHER GOD, PLEASE HELP ME NEVER TO WORRY ABOUT WEALTH. I DON'T WANT MY LIFE GOALS TO BE ABOUT MONEY; I WANT THEM TO BE ABOUT SERVING YOU AND DOING THE GOOD THINGS YOU HAVE PLANNED FOR ME! I TRUST THAT YOU WILL PROVIDE FOR ME AND BLESS ME AS YOU SEE FIT. AMEN.

FOCUS ON THE BOOK OF NEHEMIAH

"The people you rescued by your great power and strong hand are your servants. O Lord, please hear my prayer! Listen to the prayers of those of us who delight in honoring you."

NEHEMIAH 1:10–11 NLT

When our overactive minds need worthwhile things to think about, we can focus on learning more from the book of Nehemiah. In this book, we learn a lot about a Jewish man named Nehemiah who served as the cupbearer for the Persian king Artaxerxes. His job was to taste all the king's food and drink before the king did to make sure no one was trying to poison the king.

Nehemiah found favor with the king, so when Nehemiah wanted to go back to his homeland and help build the walls around Jerusalem, the king allowed him to go. Nehemiah organized and led a team of builders, and within fifty-two days they were able to rebuild the city's walls. That was incredibly quick for such a big job, and it showed how God's power was clearly at work. Nehemiah loved and respected God with all his heart, and he continued to help the Jewish people to want to honor and obey Him in all things.

FATHER, THANK YOU FOR EACH BOOK IN THE BIBLE. HELP ME AS I LEARN FROM THE BOOK OF NEHEMIAH AND KEEP COMING BACK TO IT IN THE FUTURE. TEACH ME HOW TO APPLY ITS TRUTH TO MY LIFE AND TO SHARE IT WITH OTHERS. PLEASE DRAW ME CLOSER TO YOU THROUGH YOUR WORD. AMEN.

BE PROUD OF WHAT THE LORD HAS DONE

If anyone wants to be proud, he should be proud of what the Lord has done.

2 Corinthians 10:17 NLV

Sometimes the root cause of overthinking and anxiety is pride. We worry too much about appearing like we never mess up or make mistakes. Or we feel pressure to look perfect and wear the latest fashions or name brands and have the most updated homes. Or we feel like we need to keep up and be the best—or at least better than those around us—in our work and other activities.

God's Word tells us many times that pride is a sin that can get us into lots of trouble. The only area where we should be proud about anything is being proud of what God does. He is the one we should point others to as perfect, certainly not ourselves. No person is perfect, and when we can be humble and honestly admit our mistakes and weaknesses and the ways we don't measure up, we sincerely help show others the need for everyone to have faith in our perfect Savior Jesus Christ.

FATHER GOD, HELP ME GET RID OF SELF-PRIDE. I WANT TO BE PROUD OF YOU, AND YOU ALONE. HELP ME TO SEE HOW EVERY GOOD THING I EVER DO ULTIMATELY COMES FROM YOU! HELP ME TO SHOW OTHERS BOTH MY NEED AND THEIR NEED FOR JESUS. AMEN.

FOCUS ON THE BOOK OF ESTHER

Mordecai sent this reply to Esther: "Don't think for a moment that because you're in the palace you will escape when all other Jews are killed. If you keep quiet at a time like this, deliverance and relief for the Jews will arise from some other place, but you and your relatives will die. Who knows if perhaps you were made queen for just such a time as this?"

ESTHER 4:13–14 NLT

When our overactive minds need worthwhile things to think about, we can focus on learning more from the book of Esther. In this book, we learn that when King Xerxes of Persia began searching for a new queen, he chose Esther. She was a Jewish woman, but she had kept her family history a secret.

A high official named Haman wanted all people to bow down and honor him, but Esther's cousin Mordecai refused to bow down to anyone but God. Because of this, Haman was filled with hate for Jewish people, and he convinced King Xerxes to order a decree to have them all killed. But Esther had great courage, and she asked the king to have mercy on the Jews. When you read the whole story of Esther in the Bible, you learn how she let God work through her to save her entire nation of people.

FATHER, THANK YOU FOR EACH BOOK IN THE BIBLE. HELP ME AS I LEARN FROM THE BOOK OF ESTHER AND KEEP COMING BACK TO IT IN THE FUTURE. TEACH ME HOW TO APPLY ITS TRUTH TO MY LIFE AND TO SHARE IT WITH OTHERS. PLEASE DRAW ME CLOSER TO YOU THROUGH YOUR WORD. AMEN.

FEELING REJECTION

All praise to God, the Father of our Lord Jesus Christ. God is our merciful Father and the source of all comfort. He comforts us in all our troubles so that we can comfort others. When they are troubled, we will be able to give them the same comfort God has given us. For the more we suffer for Christ, the more God will shower us with his comfort through Christ.

2 CORINTHIANS 1:3–5 NLT

Feeling rejection in this life is inevitable at times. It can hurt badly, and we can spend far too much time uselessly overthinking it.

In painful, confusing times of rejection, the best thing we can do is pour out our hearts to God in prayer. He wants to pull us close, comfort us, and remind us that Jesus knows exactly what it's like to feel rejected. When we share with Him in suffering, we're bonding with Him, and He's strengthening our faith and character. He's also storing up rewards for us in heaven.

We can keep trusting and loving our Savior and keep praying, no matter what rejection and suffering we go through. He is good through it all, and He is working to make all things right!

DEAR JESUS, WHEN I FEEL REJECTED, REMIND ME HOW REJECTED YOU WERE. BUT IN YOUR REJECTION AND SUFFERING, GOD WAS WORKING TO SAVE THE WORLD. REMIND ME THAT WHEN I AM REJECTED AND SUFFERING TOO, YOU ARE WORKING IN WAYS I DON'T UNDERSTAND. PLEASE COMFORT ME AND STRENGTHEN MY FAITH AS YOU WORK BEHIND THE SCENES! AMEN.

FOCUS ON THE BOOK OF JOB

[Job] said, "Naked I came from my mother's womb, and naked shall I return. The Lord *gave, and the* Lord *has taken away; blessed be the name of the* Lord*."*

Job 1:21 ESV

When our overactive minds need worthwhile things to think about, we can focus on learning more from the book of Job. It tells of a very rich man from the land of Uz who had great faith in God. He had a wife and a large family and lots of livestock and was called the greatest man among all the people of the East. But then God allowed Satan to take everything from Job and cause him to suffer. Job loved and praised and followed God anyway—at first. But then he began to question and blame God. So God had to remind Job of His great power and goodness. Job prayed for forgiveness, and God listened and forgave him and then restored to Job all he had lost plus much more. Job's story helps us gain wisdom to endure our own sufferings.

FATHER, THANK YOU FOR EACH BOOK IN THE BIBLE. HELP ME AS I LEARN FROM THE BOOK OF JOB AND KEEP COMING BACK TO IT IN THE FUTURE. TEACH ME HOW TO APPLY ITS TRUTH TO MY LIFE AND TO SHARE IT WITH OTHERS. PLEASE DRAW ME CLOSER TO YOU THROUGH YOUR WORD. AMEN.

WONDERING WHY

We know that we are children of God and that the world around us is under the control of the evil one. And we know that the Son of God has come, and he has given us understanding so that we can know the true God. And now we live in fellowship with the true God because we live in fellowship with his Son, Jesus Christ. He is the only true God, and he is eternal life. Dear children, keep away from anything that might take God's place in your hearts.

1 JOHN 5:19–21 NLT

We could overthink endlessly, as we stress and wonder why evil things happen in this world. It's heartbreaking, but ultimately it's because the whole world is under the power of the devil.

But all of us who believe in Jesus as Savior belong to God, and the devil can never defeat us. The devil can attack us and hurt us, but God gives us life that lasts forever, no matter what! We should never want to follow any type of false god who will lead us astray in the ways of the devil.

FATHER GOD, THE DEVIL'S WAYS AND THE EVIL THINGS OF THIS WORLD ARE SCARY AND STRESSFUL, BUT I TRUST THAT WITH JESUS AS MY SAVIOR, NO MATTER WHAT HAPPENS TO ME, YOU GIVE ME LIFE THAT LASTS FOREVER! PLEASE HELP ME TO SHARE THIS TRUTH WITH OTHERS SO THAT THEY CAN BE SAVED FROM THE EVIL IN THIS WORLD TOO. AMEN.

FOCUS ON THE BOOK OF PSALMS

LORD, my heart is not proud; my eyes are not haughty. I don't concern myself with matters too great or too awesome for me to grasp. Instead, I have calmed and quieted myself, like a weaned child who no longer cries for its mother's milk. Yes, like a weaned child is my soul within me. O Israel, put your hope in the LORD—now and always.

PSALM 131 NLT

When our overactive minds need worthwhile things to think about, we can focus on learning more from the book of Psalms. At 150 chapters, it's the longest book of the Bible and contains a huge collection of songs and poems and writings in which the authors are praising and worshipping, praying and crying out to God with all kinds of relatable emotions. As we read the psalms, they can lead us in meaningful praise and worship and help guide us in our prayers and requests to God.

FATHER, THANK YOU FOR EACH BOOK IN THE BIBLE. HELP ME AS I LEARN FROM THE BOOK OF PSALMS AND KEEP COMING BACK TO IT IN THE FUTURE. TEACH ME HOW TO APPLY ITS TRUTH TO MY LIFE AND TO SHARE IT WITH OTHERS. PLEASE DRAW ME CLOSER TO YOU THROUGH YOUR WORD. AMEN.

ONLY FOR A LITTLE WHILE

In his kindness God called you to share in his eternal glory by means of Christ Jesus. So after you have suffered a little while, he will restore, support, and strengthen you, and he will place you on a firm foundation. All power to him forever! Amen.

1 PETER 5:10–11 NLT

We've all experienced many types of worries and hurts in this world—little ones and big ones. But God's Word promises that all kinds of suffering and pain are just for a little while as we wait for perfection in heaven. Meanwhile God will keep us on the right path and give us strength to deal with the stress and hardships of this life. No difficulty can ever overpower us, because we trust that God has power over everything.

DEAR JESUS, I HATE THE STRESSFUL AND PAINFUL THINGS OF THIS WORLD, BUT I LOVE THAT YOU HAVE COMPLETE POWER OVER ALL OF THEM. I BELIEVE THAT YOU ARE WORKING TO MAKE ALL THINGS PERFECT AND WORRY-FREE FOREVER IN HEAVEN—FOR ME AND ALL WHO TRUST IN YOU. AMEN.

FOCUS ON THE BOOK OF PROVERBS

The proverbs of Solomon, son of David, king of Israel: To know wisdom and instruction, to understand words of insight, to receive instruction in wise dealing, in righteousness, justice, and equity; to give prudence to the simple, knowledge and discretion to the youth—Let the wise hear and increase in learning, and the one who understands obtain guidance, to understand a proverb and a saying, the words of the wise and their riddles. The fear of the LORD *is the beginning of knowledge; fools despise wisdom and instruction.*

PROVERBS 1:1–7 ESV

When our overactive minds need worthwhile things to think about, we can focus on learning more from the book of Proverbs, which is all about wisdom. It's a collection of short sayings and thoughts and principles to help people of all ages in all kinds of situations choose right instead of wrong by following God's good ways.

Since most of our months have thirty-one days, it's awesome that there are thirty-one chapters. It's a wonderful habit to read one chapter of Proverbs every day of the month and then start all over again the next month.

FATHER, THANK YOU FOR EACH BOOK IN THE BIBLE. HELP ME AS I LEARN FROM THE BOOK OF PROVERBS AND KEEP COMING BACK TO IT IN THE FUTURE. TEACH ME HOW TO APPLY ITS TRUTH TO MY LIFE AND TO SHARE IT WITH OTHERS. PLEASE DRAW ME CLOSER TO YOU THROUGH YOUR WORD. AMEN.

DO YOUR BEST TO LIVE AT PEACE WITH EVERYONE

Do not repay anyone evil for evil. Be careful to do what is right in the eyes of everyone. If it is possible, as far as it depends on you, live at peace with everyone. Do not take revenge, my dear friends.

ROMANS 12:17–19 NIV

Are you always at peace with your family and friends? Probably not. And that can cause lots of worries and stress. Any relationship is going to have some conflict, and that's okay if we handle it wisely! Physical fighting is not good, but conflict with wisdom behind it can be helpful as we learn to work out problems in our relationships. We truly need conflict sometimes.

But we shouldn't want to *stay* in conflict; we should work through it until there is peace again. James 4:1 (NLV) says, "What starts wars and fights among you? Is it not because you want many things and are fighting to have them?" This shows us that so many of our conflicts are caused by selfishness, and when we are willing to work to make peace, we should be willing to admit our own selfishness and mistakes even as we point out selfishness and mistakes in others.

FATHER GOD, PLEASE SHOW ME HOW YOU WANT ME TO DO MY BEST TO WORK THROUGH CONFLICT WISELY AND LIVE IN PEACE WITH EVERYONE. AMEN.

FORGIVE LIKE GOD FORGIVES

"If you forgive those who sin against you, your heavenly Father will forgive you. But if you refuse to forgive others, your Father will not forgive your sins."

MATTHEW 6:14–15 NLT

When we're praying and wanting God to pay attention, we need God's forgiveness of our sins. And we also need to forgive others for the sins they have done that have hurt us. God loves giving grace and forgiveness, and He wants us to imitate Him. We should be so grateful for His forgiveness of all our own sin that we want to give generous forgiveness to others.

This can be extremely hard to do. But with God's power working in us, offering forgiveness is always possible. Even if the ones who have hurt us don't ever seem sorry and we might never be in close relationship again, we can still ask God to help us let go of the anger and pain they caused and trust that He is working all things out for good.

FATHER GOD, I NEED YOUR HELP TO IMITATE FORGIVENESS THE WAY YOU GIVE IT SO KINDLY AND GENEROUSLY. I CANNOT DO IT ON MY OWN. IT'S WAY TOO HARD. BUT I CAN DO IT WITH YOUR HELP, AND FOR THAT I'M GRATEFUL. AMEN.

CRY OUT AND CALM DOWN

I cried to the Lord in my trouble, and He answered me and put me in a good place.

PSALM 118:5 NLV

When we're overwhelmed and feel like we're in a whole lot of trouble, we need to stop to think about how God has helped us out of trouble in the past. That can help us calm down and trust that He will do so again.

Psalm 118 encourages us that we can always cry out to God in our troubles, and He will help us get back into a good, safe place. It goes on to say, "The Lord is with me. I will not be afraid of what man can do to me. The Lord is with me. He is my Helper. I will watch those lose who fight against me. It is better to trust in the Lord than to trust in man. It is better to trust in the Lord than to trust in rulers" (Psalm 118:6–9 NLV).

FATHER GOD, I TRUST YOU MORE THAN ANY PERSON OR LEADER. I KNOW YOU ARE ALWAYS WITH ME, AND I DON'T NEED TO BE AFRAID OF ANYONE. WHEN I'M IN TROUBLE, PLEASE HELP ME TO GET OUT OF IT AND INTO A GOOD, SAFE PLACE. THANK YOU! AMEN.

FOCUS ON THE BOOK OF ECCLESIASTES

The end of the matter; all has been heard. Fear God and keep his commandments, for this is the whole duty of man. For God will bring every deed into judgment, with every secret thing, whether good or evil.

Ecclesiastes 12:13–14 esv

When our overactive minds need worthwhile things to think about, we can focus on learning more from the book of Ecclesiastes. The author was most likely King Solomon, the king with whom God was so pleased when he asked for wisdom. But King Solomon didn't continue using wisdom later in his life, and some Bible experts think he wrote Ecclesiastes to help teach other people the lessons he learned from his bad choices.

We are wise when we listen and learn from those who have made mistakes and learned from them. Our listening will hopefully help us avoid making those same mistakes.

FATHER, THANK YOU FOR EACH BOOK IN THE BIBLE. HELP ME AS I LEARN FROM THE BOOK OF ECCLESIASTES AND KEEP COMING BACK TO IT IN THE FUTURE. TEACH ME HOW TO APPLY ITS TRUTH TO MY LIFE AND TO SHARE IT WITH OTHERS. PLEASE DRAW ME CLOSER TO YOU THROUGH YOUR WORD. AMEN.

DON'T OVERTHINK BAD CHOICES, PART 1

And Jesus said, "There was a man who had two sons. The younger son said to his father, 'Father, let me have the part of the family riches that will be coming to me.' Then the father divided all that he owned between his two sons. Soon after that the younger son took all that had been given to him and went to another country far away. There he spent all he had on wild and foolish living. When all his money was spent, he was hungry. There was no food in the land. He went to work for a man in this far away country. His work was to feed pigs. He was so hungry he was ready to eat the outside part of the ears of the corn the pigs ate because no one gave him anything. He began to think about what he had done."

LUKE 15:11–17 NLV

We all make bad choices from time to time, and sometimes we overthink and continuously beat ourselves up because of them. But in this parable, Jesus was teaching about God's great love for us, even when we make bad choices, just like the younger son in this story. If you find that you're beating yourself up over a terrible choice, give it to God. He'll be happy to take that burden from you!

FATHER GOD, PLEASE HELP ME TO THINK ABOUT MY CHOICES AND ADMIT TO YOU WHEN I'VE SINNED AGAINST YOU. PLEASE FORGIVE ME AND HELP ME NOT TO MAKE THE SAME BAD CHOICES AGAIN IN THE FUTURE. HELP ME TO TRUST IN YOUR GRACE AND NOT BEAT MYSELF UP FOR WHAT YOU HAVE ALREADY FORGIVEN ME FOR. AMEN.

DON'T OVERTHINK BAD CHOICES, PART 2

"I will get up and go to my father. I will say to him, 'Father, I have sinned against heaven and against you.'"

LUKE 15:18 NLV

The parable Jesus told continues:

> *"The son got up and went to his father. While he was yet a long way off, his father saw him. The father was full of loving-pity for him. He ran and threw his arms around him and kissed him. The son said to him, 'Father, I have sinned against heaven and against you. I am not good enough to be called your son.' But the father said to the workmen he owned, 'Hurry! Get the best coat and put it on him. Put a ring on his hand and shoes on his feet. Bring the calf that is fat and kill it. Let us eat and be glad. For my son was dead and now he is alive again. He was lost and now he is found. Let us eat and have a good time.'" (Luke 15:20–24 NLV)*

God loves us just like the father in the story loved his sons. He doesn't want to hold our sins against us. When we confess them to Him and come back to close relationship with Him, He feels like throwing us a celebration party too!

FATHER GOD, THANK YOU SO MUCH FOR YOUR AMAZING GRACE TO FORGIVE MY SINS. AMEN.

FOCUS ON THE SONG OF SOLOMON

Let him kiss me with the kisses of his mouth—for your love is more delightful than wine. Pleasing is the fragrance of your perfumes; your name is like perfume poured out. No wonder the young women love you! Take me away with you—let us hurry! Let the king bring me into his chambers.

SONG OF SONGS 1:2–4 NIV

When our overactive minds need worthwhile things to think about, we can focus on learning more from the book of Song of Solomon, or Song of Songs, as it's also called. It's a book about the beauty of married love. Some Bible experts think it was written (either by Solomon or about him) to compare married love with how much God loves His people.

FATHER, THANK YOU FOR EACH BOOK IN THE BIBLE. HELP ME AS I LEARN FROM THE BOOK OF SONG OF SOLOMON AND KEEP COMING BACK TO IT IN THE FUTURE. TEACH ME HOW TO APPLY ITS TRUTH TO MY LIFE AND TO SHARE IT WITH OTHERS. PLEASE DRAW ME CLOSER TO YOU THROUGH YOUR WORD. AMEN.

STRENGTH LIKE A LION

Those who are right with God have as much strength of heart as a lion.

PROVERBS 28:1 NLV

We overthinkers sometimes look to the future feeling like we can't handle any more challenges or hardships that will inevitably come our way. But God's Word promises us supernatural strength, so of course we can deal with them and even thrive during them!

Trusting in Jesus as the one who took away our sins when He died on the cross is what makes us right with God. And if we believe that and are living for Jesus, we have as much strength of heart as a lion. Our hearts and emotions can deal with any hard thing because we know that real strength comes from God alone. He is in us through His Holy Spirit. We can face any fear or worry without running away, because of God's great power in us and love for us.

FATHER GOD, I TRUST IN JESUS AS MY SAVIOR FROM SIN, AND I'M SO GRATEFUL THAT MAKES ME RIGHT WITH YOU! THANK YOU FOR MAKING ME STRONG AND CAPABLE WITH YOUR AWESOME POWER. AMEN.

FOCUS ON THE BOOK OF ISAIAH

Surely he took up our pain and bore our suffering, yet we considered him punished by God, stricken by him, and afflicted. But he was pierced for our transgressions, he was crushed for our iniquities; the punishment that brought us peace was on him, and by his wounds we are healed. We all, like sheep, have gone astray, each of us has turned to our own way; and the LORD has laid on him the iniquity of us all.

ISAIAH 53:4–6 NIV

When our overactive minds need worthwhile things to think about, we can focus on learning more from the book of Isaiah, which is the first in a series of seventeen books written by prophets. They are books that not only give warnings about God's judgment but give encouragement with the promises of God's salvation and forgiveness and the way He rescues when people turn back to Him.

Isaiah is extra special among the prophetic books because it has more prophecies telling about our Savior, Jesus Christ, than any of the others.

FATHER, THANK YOU FOR EACH BOOK IN THE BIBLE. HELP ME AS I LEARN FROM THE BOOK OF ISAIAH AND KEEP COMING BACK TO IT IN THE FUTURE. TEACH ME HOW TO APPLY ITS TRUTH TO MY LIFE AND TO SHARE IT WITH OTHERS. PLEASE DRAW ME CLOSER TO YOU THROUGH YOUR WORD. AMEN.

BE ON GUARD

Guard your heart above all else, for it determines the course of your life.

PROVERBS 4:23 NLT

If we feel overwhelmed with racing thoughts and worries some of the time, that's understandable. But what if we feel that way *all* the time? Not good! If that's the case, we need to figure out where constant confusing and overwhelming anxiety is coming from and how to communicate about it, plus hopefully work through what's causing it so we can be well again.

Sometimes we need to ask trusted loved ones for help and be totally honest about our overwhelming thoughts and feelings. And we can't ever forget that God knows our hearts and minds best of all, and He can help us with everything we think and feel. We can constantly pray to Him and ask Him to give great wisdom and care when it comes to our thoughts and emotions and actions and how they're all connected.

FATHER GOD, SOMETIMES I'M THINKING AND WORRYING SO MUCH THAT I'M NOT SURE WHAT TO DO WITH IT ALL. YOU KNOW MY HEART AND EVERY THOUGHT AND FEELING EVEN BETTER THAN I DO. CAN YOU PLEASE HELP ME SORT THEM OUT AND COMMUNICATE THEM WELL SO OTHERS CAN HELP ME? THANK YOU! AMEN.

FOCUS ON THE BOOK OF JEREMIAH

These are the words of Jeremiah son of Hilkiah, one of the priests from the town of Anathoth in the land of Benjamin. The LORD *first gave messages to Jeremiah during the thirteenth year of the reign of Josiah son of Amon, king of Judah. The* LORD*'s messages continued throughout the reign of King Jehoiakim, Josiah's son, until the eleventh year of the reign of King Zedekiah, another of Josiah's sons.*

JEREMIAH 1:1–3 NLT

When our overactive minds need worthwhile things to think about, we can focus on learning more from the book of Jeremiah. After King Josiah died, the nation of Judah had turned almost completely away from God. So, in his book, the prophet Jeremiah warned the people of Judah of the punishment and the suffering that were about to come their way because of their rejection of God and His good ways.

This book of the Bible reminds us never to reject God and never to stop obeying Him. He always wants what's best for us.

FATHER, THANK YOU FOR EACH BOOK IN THE BIBLE. HELP ME AS I LEARN FROM THE BOOK OF JEREMIAH AND KEEP COMING BACK TO IT IN THE FUTURE. TEACH ME HOW TO APPLY ITS TRUTH TO MY LIFE AND TO SHARE IT WITH OTHERS. PLEASE DRAW ME CLOSER TO YOU THROUGH YOUR WORD. AMEN.

DON'T HINDER COMMUNICATION

If I had not confessed the sin in my heart, the Lord would not have listened.

PSALM 66:18 NLT

To better manage our overthinking, we need to have good prayer and communication with God. And to have good communication with God, we can't be holding on to sin. We know that in any relationship, if we have unresolved conflict going on, it hinders our communication in that particular relationship—and it also hinders our communication with God.

We need to do our best to keep ourselves away from sin so that God doesn't tune out our prayers. If we've asked Jesus to be our Savior, then we are right with Him because of His grace. But that doesn't mean we should purposefully do anything that goes against God's Word again and again.

Romans 5:20–6:2 (NLT) says, "God's law was given so that all people could see how sinful they were. But as people sinned more and more, God's wonderful grace became more abundant. So just as sin ruled over all people and brought them to death, now God's wonderful grace rules instead, giving us right standing with God and resulting in eternal life through Jesus Christ our Lord. Well then, should we keep on sinning so that God can show us more and more of his wonderful grace? Of course not!"

....

....

....

....

....

....

FATHER GOD, I KNOW THAT BECAUSE JESUS IS MY SAVIOR, YOU TAKE AWAY MY SIN. BUT EVEN THOUGH I AM SAVED, I DON'T WANT TO PURPOSEFULLY GO AGAINST YOUR WORD. I LOVE YOU AND WANT TO PLEASE YOU, AND I NEVER WANT TO HINDER COMMUNICATION WITH YOU. AMEN.

FOCUS ON THE BOOK OF LAMENTATIONS

Jerusalem's gates have sunk into the ground. He has smashed their locks and bars. Her kings and princes have been exiled to distant lands; her law has ceased to exist. Her prophets receive no more visions from the Lord. *The leaders of beautiful Jerusalem sit on the ground in silence. They are clothed in burlap and throw dust on their heads. The young women of Jerusalem hang their heads in shame. I have cried until the tears no longer come; my heart is broken. My spirit is poured out in agony as I see the desperate plight of my people.*

LAMENTATIONS 2:9–11 NLT

When our overactive minds need worthwhile things to think about, we can focus on learning more from the book of Lamentations, which is written by the prophet Jeremiah. The word *lamentation* means an expression of sorrow. In the book of Lamentations, Jeremiah was writing down all of his sadness about the way the city of Jerusalem had been destroyed (just like God had told him to warn about in his first book) because of the ways the people had turned away from God.

FATHER, THANK YOU FOR EACH BOOK IN THE BIBLE. HELP ME AS I LEARN FROM THE BOOK OF LAMENTATIONS AND KEEP COMING BACK TO IT IN THE FUTURE. TEACH ME HOW TO APPLY ITS TRUTH TO MY LIFE AND TO SHARE IT WITH OTHERS. PLEASE DRAW ME CLOSER TO YOU THROUGH YOUR WORD. AMEN.

FOR THOSE WHO LOVE GOD

And we know that for those who love God all things work together for good, for those who are called according to his purpose.

Romans 8:28 ESV

The Bible promises that God makes everything work together for the good of those who love Him. But that doesn't always seem to make sense—no matter how hard we think about it! Like when we're blindsided by the loss of a job. Or, far worse, when we've prayed so much for healing from an illness for a loved one but that loved one dies. It's heartbreaking and confusing.

Just because we're disappointed and hurting and can't understand, that doesn't mean God has changed or His promises aren't true. We have to choose to trust Him even more when we don't understand Him. We have to trust that His thoughts and ways are much higher than ours (Isaiah 55:8–9) and that He is working in ways we will not understand in this world. But He promises that someday we will understand, and so we keep the faith by praying to Him and believing Him and learning from Him.

FATHER GOD, WHEN I'M HURTING AND CONFUSED, PLEASE HOLD ME EXTRA CLOSE AND SHOW ME YOUR LOVE IN UNEXPECTED WAYS. I DON'T WANT TO TURN AWAY FROM YOU JUST BECAUSE I DON'T UNDERSTAND YOU. AMEN.

BE CONTENT WHATEVER THE CIRCUMSTANCES

I have learned to be content whatever the circumstances. I know what it is to be in need, and I know what it is to have plenty. I have learned the secret of being content in any and every situation, whether well fed or hungry, whether living in plenty or in want. I can do all this through him who gives me strength.

PHILIPPIANS 4:11–13 NIV

In a world with so many cool things—plus TV and the internet and social media that tell us all about those things instantly—we often struggle to be content with the life we've been given. And that desire for more can cause a lot of unnecessary overthinking and anxiety. It's tempting to look at other people's stuff and all the fun stuff they do, and then want what they have and do what they do. All that comparison makes it hard to be content in our personal situation.

We need to pray hard against envy and greed, and we need to remember how to be happy and content. We simply must remember that we can do all things through Christ who gives us strength. Because He helps us, we can be happy and endure when we have little, and we can be happy and give thanks when we have plenty. Jesus gives us strength no matter what, and trusting in Him is where real contentment comes from!

FATHER GOD, HELP ME TO BE CONTENT WITH WHATEVER YOU DECIDE TO BLESS ME WITH. HELP ME TO TRUST IN YOUR STRENGTH AND THE WAYS YOU PROVIDE, NO MATTER WHAT I DO OR DON'T HAVE. AMEN.

FOCUS ON THE BOOK OF EZEKIEL

"As surely as I live, says the Sovereign LORD, I take no pleasure in the death of wicked people. I only want them to turn from their wicked ways so they can live. Turn! Turn from your wickedness, O people of Israel! Why should you die?"

EZEKIEL 33:11 NLT

When our overactive minds need worthwhile things to think about, we can focus on learning more from the book of Ezekiel, who was a prophet whose name means "strengthened by God." He preached to the people of his day about God's judgment and salvation. Sometimes God told Ezekiel to do some extremely bizarre things to demonstrate the warnings God wanted the people to hear. For example, when Ezekiel was told to lie on his left side for 390 days, that was to show the nation of Israel it would be punished for 390 years for turning away from God. However, as Ezekiel 33:11 shows us, God is never happy when people are punished for their sins. He wants people to turn away from them and let Him give them the best kind of life with faith in and obedience to Him.

FATHER, THANK YOU FOR EACH BOOK IN THE BIBLE. HELP ME AS I LEARN FROM THE BOOK OF EZEKIEL AND KEEP COMING BACK TO IT IN THE FUTURE. TEACH ME HOW TO APPLY ITS TRUTH TO MY LIFE AND TO SHARE IT WITH OTHERS. PLEASE DRAW ME CLOSER TO YOU THROUGH YOUR WORD. AMEN.

WHEN PLANS CHANGE

The heart of man plans his way, but the LORD establishes his steps.

PROVERBS 16:9 ESV

Sometimes we make good plans but they unexpectedly change, and that can really frustrate an overthinker! We wonder why God doesn't help things turn out the way we thought they would or the way we worked so hard toward. In those times, we must remember that God sees and knows all. He sees and knows far above and beyond what we can see and understand.

It's okay to make our plans (asking for God's wisdom and direction as we do), but we need to work toward them while also holding them loosely, praying like this:

FATHER GOD, I NEED YOUR WISDOM AND DIRECTION AS I MAKE PLANS. PLEASE HELP MY PLANS TO HONOR YOU AND FOLLOW YOUR WILL. BUT PLEASE ALSO HELP ME TO REMEMBER THAT YOU SEE THINGS ABOUT MY PLANS THAT I DON'T, AND SOMETIMES YOU CHANGE THEM OR LET CHANGES HAPPEN TO THEM. I MIGHT NOT ALWAYS UNDERSTAND THE DETAILS, BUT I TRUST YOU ARE DOING WHAT IS BEST AND WILL MAKE EVERYTHING RIGHT SOMEDAY. AMEN.

CAREFUL

Test everything and do not let good things get away from you.
Keep away from everything that even looks like sin.
1 Thessalonians 5:21–22 nlv

We have many options in movies, TV, music, social media, and entertainment these days. And all those things can be a huge source of anxiety and temptation to sin if we're not careful. We need to pray for wisdom about what we watch, listen to, read, and participate in on the internet.

We should strive to be able to say, like David did in Psalm 101:2–3 (nlt), "I will be careful to live a blameless life—when will you come to help me? I will lead a life of integrity in my own home. I will refuse to look at anything vile and vulgar."

LORD, PLEASE HELP ME AS I MAKE ENTERTAINMENT AND SOCIAL MEDIA CHOICES. SOMETIMES THE OPTIONS SEEM SO OUT OF CONTROL, AND IT'S SURE NOT A POPULAR CHOICE TO BE CAREFUL! BUT I LOVE YOU, AND I WANT TO STAY AWAY FROM THE THINGS THAT CAUSE ME ANXIETY AND FROM ANYTHING THAT CAUSES ME TO SIN AND DISAPPOINT YOU. AMEN.

FOCUS ON THE BOOK OF DANIEL

God gave these four young men an unusual aptitude for understanding every aspect of literature and wisdom. And God gave Daniel the special ability to interpret the meanings of visions and dreams.

DANIEL 1:17 NLT

When our overactive minds need worthwhile things to think about, we can focus on learning more from the book of Daniel, which contains several of the most amazing and well-known Bible stories—like the story of when Daniel was thrown into the lions' den because he refused to stop praying to God. And the story of Daniel's friends Shadrach, Meshach, and Abednego, who were thrown into a fiery furnace because they would not bow down to a false god. These stories and others about faithfulness to God, even in the worst and scariest of situations, help us to be strong and courageous in our faith as well.

FATHER, THANK YOU FOR EACH BOOK IN THE BIBLE. HELP ME AS I LEARN FROM THE BOOK OF DANIEL AND KEEP COMING BACK TO IT IN THE FUTURE. TEACH ME HOW TO APPLY ITS TRUTH TO MY LIFE AND TO SHARE IT WITH OTHERS. PLEASE DRAW ME CLOSER TO YOU THROUGH YOUR WORD. AMEN.

THE LORD DELIGHTS IN TRUSTWORTHY PEOPLE

The Lord *detests lying lips, but he delights in people who are trustworthy.*

Proverbs 12:22 niv

People who lie must do a lot of extra thinking to keep their made-up stories straight. Being honest about everything helps us avoid all kinds of stress and anxiety and overwhelming thoughts in our lives.

If we make honesty and integrity top priorities, we will be known as trustworthy. The bosses and leaders in our lives notice consistent honesty, and good ones usually want to reward us and give new opportunities because of it. Luke 16:10–12 (nlv) says, "He that is faithful with little things is faithful with big things also. He that is not honest with little things is not honest with big things. If you have not been faithful with riches of this world, who will trust you with true riches? If you have not been faithful in that which belongs to another person, who will give you things to have as your own?"

FATHER GOD, I WANT YOU TO DELIGHT IN ME BECAUSE I ALWAYS TELL THE TRUTH. I WANT TO BE WISE AND HONEST AND TRUSTWORTHY IN ALL THINGS. AMEN.

LOOK FOR HIS COMING

We are to be looking for the great hope and the coming of our great God and the One Who saves, Christ Jesus.

TITUS 2:13 NLV

One day Jesus will return and put an end to every worry and stress we have on this earth. We should always be watching for Him because He promised to come back! The idea of Jesus returning might sound a little scary because it will be unlike anything any person has ever experienced. But for those who love and trust Him, His return will be wonderful, and we should have great excitement and hope about it!

Mark 13:24–27 (NLV) says, "After those days of much trouble and pain and sorrow are over, the sun will get dark. The moon will not give light. The stars will fall from the sky. The powers in the heavens will be shaken. Then they will see the Son of Man coming in the clouds with great power and shining-greatness. He will send His angels. They will gather together God's people from the four winds. They will come from one end of the earth to the other end of heaven."

DEAR JESUS, I'M WATCHING AND WAITING FOR YOU TO RETURN AND GATHER YOUR PEOPLE, INCLUDING ME! I LOVE YOU AND TRUST YOU! AMEN.

FOCUS ON THE BOOK OF HOSEA

"Come, let us return to the Lord. He has hurt us but He will heal us. He has cut us but He will cover the sore. After two days He will give us new life. He will raise us up on the third day, that we may live before Him. So keep on trying to know the Lord. His coming to us is as sure as the rising of the sun. He will come to us like the rain, like the spring rain giving water to the earth."

HOSEA 6:1–3 NLV

When our overactive minds need worthwhile things to think about, we can focus on learning more from the book of Hosea, which tells how the prophet Hosea—whose name means "salvation"—obeyed God's instructions to marry a woman named Gomer, who was unfaithful to him. But when Gomer ran away, God told Hosea to go and win her back. God used this to illustrate how even while the people of Israel were unfaithful to God, He still loved them and wanted to win them back to Him.

FATHER, THANK YOU FOR EACH BOOK IN THE BIBLE. HELP ME AS I LEARN FROM THE BOOK OF HOSEA AND KEEP COMING BACK TO IT IN THE FUTURE. TEACH ME HOW TO APPLY ITS TRUTH TO MY LIFE AND TO SHARE IT WITH OTHERS. PLEASE DRAW ME CLOSER TO YOU THROUGH YOUR WORD. AMEN.

MARTHA WAS AN OVERTHINKER

Martha was distracted by the big dinner she was preparing. She came to Jesus and said, "Lord, doesn't it seem unfair to you that my sister just sits here while I do all the work? Tell her to come and help me." But the Lord said to her, "My dear Martha, you are worried and upset over all these details! There is only one thing worth being concerned about. Mary has discovered it, and it will not be taken away from her."

LUKE 10:40–42 NLT

Martha was an overthinker, and we can learn from how Jesus lovingly corrected her. She and her sister Mary were good friends of Jesus. One time when Jesus was coming over for dinner, Martha was keeping busy doing good things to make a nice meal and take care of Jesus. But she was worried and upset that Mary wasn't helping enough. We can relate, right?

Do you ever feel like you're the one doing all the thinking and all the work when others should also be helping you get things accomplished? It's frustrating and stressful, for sure! But in this case, Jesus gently told Martha that Mary was doing the very best thing—simply being still and focusing on Jesus and His teaching. Our worries and overthinking will be eased if we simply sit still and listen to Jesus too.

DEAR JESUS, PLEASE REMIND ME THAT FUSSING AND FRETTING OVER EVERYTHING IS NOT GOOD FOR ME. IT'S FAR MORE IMPORTANT TO SPEND TIME WITH YOU AND LISTEN TO WHAT YOU WANT TO TEACH ME. AMEN.

BE WEIRD!

Dear friends, I warn you as "temporary residents and foreigners" to keep away from worldly desires that wage war against your very souls. Be careful to live properly among your unbelieving neighbors. Then even if they accuse you of doing wrong, they will see your honorable behavior, and they will give honor to God when he judges the world.

1 PETER 2:11–12 NLT

Sometimes being a Christian feels weird—and that's a good thing, because God's Word tells us we should feel different. We don't need to overthink or worry about it!

Some versions of 1 Peter 2:11 describe Christians as being foreigners or aliens here on earth because this world is not our real home. When we believe in Jesus as Savior, we know that He will give us eternal life someday in heaven, which *is* our real home. So, we should be careful not to follow what the world says is good and popular but to follow what God says is good—which will often be very unpopular in the world. That will help show others the difference in following Jesus, and hopefully they will want to follow Him too.

Being a Christian in this world isn't always easy, but it is *always* totally worth it!

FATHER GOD, NO MATTER HOW WEIRD I FEEL, HELP ME TO FOLLOW YOUR WAYS AND WISDOM ABOVE ALL, BECAUSE I KNOW MY REAL HOME IS IN HEAVEN WITH YOU. AMEN.

FOCUS ON THE BOOK OF JOEL

"I will show powerful works in the heavens and on the earth, like blood and fire and clouds of smoke. The sun will turn dark and the moon will turn to blood before the day of the Lord. His coming will be a great and troubled day. It will be that whoever calls on the name of the Lord will be saved from the punishment of sin."

JOEL 2:30–32 NLV

When our overactive minds need worthwhile things to think about, we can focus on learning more from the book of Joel. In this book, God uses grasshoppers and His message through the prophet Joel to warn the nation of Israel to turn back to Him.

God using grasshoppers might seem ridiculous to us, but a huge swarm of them could ruin crops and cause famine and starvation and devastation for a whole nation of people. They were an example of God's judgment on sinful people and a warning of how awful it would be if armies of men instead of grasshoppers invaded the land of Israel. God wanted His people to listen to the warning so He could save and bless them.

FATHER, THANK YOU FOR EACH BOOK IN THE BIBLE. HELP ME AS I LEARN FROM THE BOOK OF JOEL AND KEEP COMING BACK TO IT IN THE FUTURE. TEACH ME HOW TO APPLY ITS TRUTH TO MY LIFE AND TO SHARE IT WITH OTHERS. PLEASE DRAW ME CLOSER TO YOU THROUGH YOUR WORD. AMEN.

KEEP ON

Teaching them more about prayer, [Jesus] used this story: "Suppose you went to a friend's house at midnight, wanting to borrow three loaves of bread. You say to him, 'A friend of mine has just arrived for a visit, and I have nothing for him to eat.' And suppose he calls out from his bedroom, 'Don't bother me. The door is locked for the night, and my family and I are all in bed. I can't help you.' But I tell you this—though he won't do it for friendship's sake, if you keep knocking long enough, he will get up and give you whatever you need because of your shameless persistence. And so I tell you, keep on asking, and you will receive what you ask for. Keep on seeking, and you will find. Keep on knocking, and the door will be opened to you. For everyone who asks, receives. Everyone who seeks, finds. And to everyone who knocks, the door will be opened."

LUKE 11:5–10 NLT

Do you wonder if God ever gets tired of your needing His help and asking for things over and over in prayer? Jesus Himself taught in the Bible that God absolutely does not! He is your all-powerful, never-tiring heavenly Father. And in Luke 11, Jesus tells you to *keep on asking*!

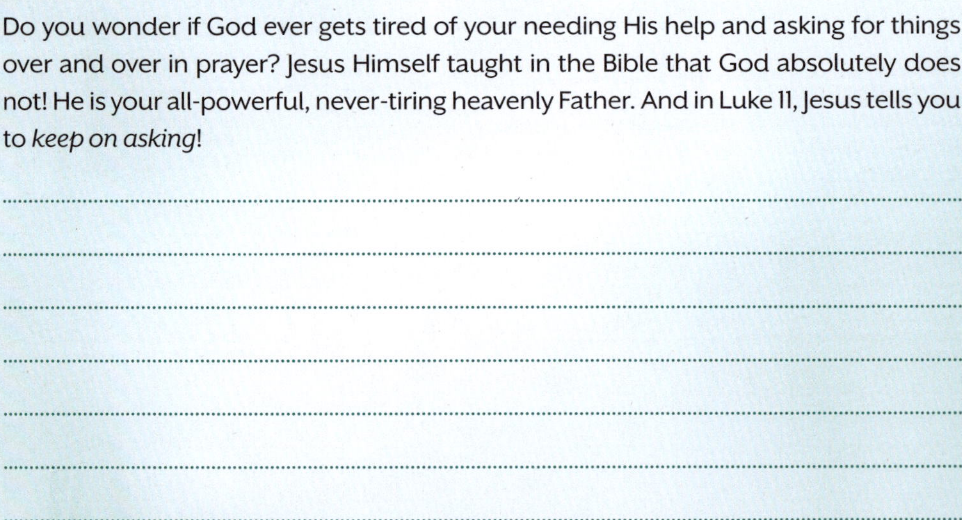

FATHER GOD, THANK YOU FOR WANTING TO HELP ME WITH MY SEEMINGLY ENDLESS OVERTHINKING. THANK YOU FOR LETTING ME ASK YOU OVER AND OVER AGAIN FOR WHAT I NEED. AMEN.

GOD GIVES WISDOM

If you need wisdom, ask our generous God, and he will give it to you. He will not rebuke you for asking. But when you ask him, be sure that your faith is in God alone. Do not waver, for a person with divided loyalty is as unsettled as a wave of the sea that is blown and tossed by the wind. Such people should not expect to receive anything from the Lord. Their loyalty is divided between God and the world, and they are unstable in everything they do.

JAMES 1:5–8 NLT

Sometimes God doesn't give what we ask for, but James 1 tells us something God is always ready to give us—*wisdom*! And we sure do need God's wisdom in this crazy world that gives us so many things to overthink and worry about. So much of what is popular in our culture goes against the good truth and guidance in God's Word.

So every day—even every *minute*!—we should ask God to give us His wisdom. We can have total faith and not even a sliver of doubt that He gives it to us. Then we can use that wisdom in every area of our lives.

FATHER GOD, THANK YOU FOR BEING SO GENEROUS WITH WISDOM. I NEED IT EVERY MINUTE, AND I'M ASKING YOU AGAIN NOW. I BELIEVE WHOLEHEARTEDLY THAT YOU GIVE IT AND GUIDE ME WITH IT. AMEN.

FOCUS ON THE BOOK OF AMOS

Now this is what the LORD says to the family of Israel: "Come back to me and live! Don't worship at the pagan altars at Bethel; don't go to the shrines at Gilgal or Beersheba. For the people of Gilgal will be dragged off into exile, and the people of Bethel will be reduced to nothing." Come back to the LORD and live!

AMOS 5:4–6 NLT

When our overactive minds need worthwhile things to think about, we can focus on learning more from the book of Amos. Amos was a shepherd and a fruit picker, just an ordinary guy who became a prophet for God. This reminds us that God can use anyone He chooses, no matter their background, to do His good works. Amos warned God's people that even though things were going well for them overall, they would soon be judged for the sin they were holding on to.

The book of Amos provides good lessons to remind us that we should look for any sin we're holding on to in our lives and confess that sin to God and ask for forgiveness. God loves to forgive and bless us when we turn back to Him.

FATHER, THANK YOU FOR EACH BOOK IN THE BIBLE. HELP ME AS I LEARN FROM THE BOOK OF AMOS AND KEEP COMING BACK TO IT IN THE FUTURE. TEACH ME HOW TO APPLY ITS TRUTH TO MY LIFE AND TO SHARE IT WITH OTHERS. PLEASE DRAW ME CLOSER TO YOU THROUGH YOUR WORD. AMEN.

OVERTHINKING IN THE WAIT TIMES

I waited patiently for the LORD to help me, and he turned to me and heard my cry.

PSALM 40:1 NLT

Overthinkers can be very impatient. Waiting for things to happen or for God to answer prayer can feel like forever and can be frustrating and stressful! But we can let God use those times to teach us to be patient and to depend on Him.

None of us thinks it's fun to listen to someone whine and complain. So we need to be careful we don't do that either while we're waiting. We can let scriptures like these fill our minds and give us wisdom about waiting when we're feeling impatient:

> *But they who wait upon the Lord will get new strength. They will rise up with wings like eagles. They will run and not get tired. They will walk and not become weak. (Isaiah 40:31 NLV)*
>
> *The Lord is good to those who wait for Him, to the one who looks for Him. (Lamentations 3:25 NLV)*

FATHER GOD, PLEASE HELP ME NOT TO WORRY AND WHINE. HELP ME INSTEAD TO WAIT LIKE YOU WANT ME TO—WITH PATIENCE AND A GOOD ATTITUDE. AMEN.

JESUS GIVES PEACE

"Peace I leave with you."
JOHN 14:27 NIV

Among many verses in the Bible that tell us not to worry or stress or fear, some of the best are Jesus' words in John 14:27 (NLV): "Peace I leave with you. My peace I give to you. I do not give peace to you as the world gives. Do not let your hearts be troubled or afraid." And Psalm 55:22 (NLV) says, "Give all your cares to the Lord and He will give you strength. He will never let those who are right with Him be shaken."

Every person and every family and every relationship and every job and every situation in life has unique challenges and troubles to face, and it's extremely hard not to endlessly overthink them. But we can train our brains to take those worrisome, racing thoughts and give them over to God in prayer. We can ask Him to replace them with His truth and peace, and then thank Him when He does.

FATHER GOD, OVERTHINKING STEALS MY PEACE AND TRUST IN YOU. PLEASE TAKE EACH WORRY FROM MY MIND AND REPLACE IT WITH A POWERFUL AND SOOTHING TRUTH ABOUT YOUR STRENGTH, YOUR PROTECTION, YOUR LOVE, AND YOUR BLESSING FOR ME. AMEN.

FOCUS ON THE BOOK OF OBADIAH

"The day is near when I, the Lord, will judge all godless nations! As you have done to Israel, so it will be done to you. All your evil deeds will fall back on your own heads."

Obadiah 15 NLT

When our overactive minds need worthwhile things to think about, we can focus on learning more from the book of Obadiah. It has only twenty-one verses total, making it the shortest book in the Old Testament. In it, God's prophet Obadiah had a message for Edom, a nasty neighbor nation of Israel. Edom would be destroyed because of how they celebrated when bad things happened to Israel and how they fought against Israel when they needed Edom's help. The book of Obadiah helps show us how protective God is of His people, and He wants to bring justice to those who mistreat them.

FATHER, THANK YOU FOR EACH BOOK IN THE BIBLE. HELP ME AS I LEARN FROM THE BOOK OF OBADIAH AND KEEP COMING BACK TO IT IN THE FUTURE. TEACH ME HOW TO APPLY ITS TRUTH TO MY LIFE AND TO SHARE IT WITH OTHERS. PLEASE DRAW ME CLOSER TO YOU THROUGH YOUR WORD. AMEN.

PRAY PROACTIVELY

"O give thanks to the Lord. Call upon His name. Let the people know what He has done. Sing to Him. Sing praises to Him. Tell of all His great works. Have joy in His holy name. Let the heart of those who look to the Lord be glad. Look to the Lord and ask for His strength. Look to Him all the time."

1 Chronicles 16:8–11 NLV

We need to pray far more than we overthink and stress over a situation. Some people pray only as a reaction to life's negative events, such as praying only when someone is already sick, rather than praying ahead of time to ask God for His help in staying healthy. Or only praying to God in emergency situations or natural disasters, rather than praying to God all the time in relationship with Him.

Of course, we should pray in reaction to life's events. We sure do need God's help in *all* circumstances! But we should also be strongly *proactive* in our prayers, building a close relationship with God while talking with Him all the time about everything—past, present, and future, and not just when we find ourselves in desperate need of His help.

FATHER GOD, PLEASE HELP ME TO PRAY PROACTIVELY. HELP ME TO BE SOMEONE WHO LOVES TO TALK TO YOU CONTINUALLY AND IN ALL SITUATIONS, NOT JUST WHEN I'M SUDDENLY IN THE MIDDLE OF AN EMERGENCY. AMEN.

THE LORD KNOWS IT ALL

O Lord, you have searched me and known me! You know when I sit down and when I rise up; you discern my thoughts from afar. You search out my path and my lying down and are acquainted with all my ways. Even before a word is on my tongue, behold, O Lord, you know it altogether. You hem me in, behind and before, and lay your hand upon me. Such knowledge is too wonderful for me; it is high; I cannot attain it.

Psalm 139:1–6 ESV

We can never keep our thoughts a secret from God. *Not ever.* Even before we say a word, God knows we're going to say it. He knows every single one of our thoughts. He knows exactly what we're doing and where and when. To some people that might seem stressful, but for those who love God and want a good relationship with Him through Jesus, it never has to be.

God loves us more than anyone else ever could! And because He sees and knows everything about us—where we are, what we're doing, what we're thinking and saying—we should feel greatly loved and protected and cared for.

FATHER GOD, THANK YOU FOR LOVING ME SO MUCH THAT YOU KNOW ALL MY THOUGHTS AND ABSOLUTELY EVERYTHING ABOUT ME! AMEN.

FOCUS ON THE BOOK OF JONAH

The word of the Lord came to Jonah son of Amittai: "Go to the great city of Nineveh and preach against it, because its wickedness has come up before me." But Jonah ran away from the Lord and headed for Tarshish. He went down to Joppa, where he found a ship bound for that port. After paying the fare, he went aboard and sailed for Tarshish to flee from the Lord.

Jonah 1:1–3 niv

When our overactive minds need worthwhile things to think about, we can focus on learning more from the book of Jonah. Jonah is one of the most well-known names in the Bible because of his time spent inside the belly of a big fish. Jonah ended up inside that fish because he didn't want to be God's prophet to Nineveh—and so he disobeyed.

We can learn much wisdom from Jonah's story, especially that even if He must take extreme, bizarre measures, God will show us how we've sinned and disobeyed and help us to get back on the path He has planned for us.

FATHER, THANK YOU FOR EACH BOOK IN THE BIBLE. HELP ME AS I LEARN FROM THE BOOK OF JONAH AND KEEP COMING BACK TO IT IN THE FUTURE. TEACH ME HOW TO APPLY ITS TRUTH TO MY LIFE AND TO SHARE IT WITH OTHERS. PLEASE DRAW ME CLOSER TO YOU THROUGH YOUR WORD. AMEN.

ALWAYS GREATER

You are from God, little children, and have overcome them; because greater is He who is in you than he who is in the world. They are from the world, therefore they speak as from the world, and the world listens to them. We are from God.

1 JOHN 4:4–6 NASB

This is a simple and powerful scripture to memorize and repeat when we're overthinking anything. Our enemy the devil is the one stirring up all kinds of evil in this world. And we will be under attack from him sometimes, in all sorts of different ways—through anxiety attacks, through someone else's cruel words or actions, through stressful times for family, through loss and sickness, and on and on.

But no matter how strong the enemy and his evil seem against us and our loved ones, they are never stronger than the power of God in us through the Holy Spirit. We can't ever forget that. We can call on God to help us be strong and peaceful and patient and to help us see how He is working and taking care of us in all situations.

FATHER GOD, DEEP DOWN I KNOW YOU ARE ALWAYS STRONGER THAN ANYTHING THAT COMES AGAINST ME. BUT I DO FORGET THAT TRUTH SOMETIMES, AND I'M SORRY. PLEASE REMIND ME AND FILL ME WITH YOUR POWER AND PEACE. AMEN.

LOVE COVERS MANY SINS

You must be the boss over your mind. Keep awake so you can pray. Most of all, have a true love for each other. Love covers many sins.

1 Peter 4:7–8 NLV

When we find ourselves fighting with a loved one and dealing with a relationship that seems broken, it's very upsetting—and it's a great source of worry and overthinking. The reason for the unresolved conflict is often because we're not being patient enough with each other, or we're not listening well, or we're letting selfishness take over.

But the conflict can be worked out and the relationship can be restored if we stay humble and ask for God's help. We can pray, "God, please forgive us and help us forgive each other, and cover our mistakes with Your love and grace." And once we pray like that, we can communicate better in peaceful ways and move forward, trying to work out what's causing our conflict and unkind words and actions.

DEAR JESUS, THANK YOU MOST OF ALL FOR YOUR GREAT LOVE. YOU COVERED ALL OUR SIN WITH YOUR BLOOD WHEN YOU TOOK SIN UPON YOURSELF AND DIED ON THE CROSS. YOU DIDN'T DESERVE TO DIE, BUT THAT'S HOW MUCH YOU LOVE US! HELP US TO IMITATE YOUR GREAT LOVE AND GRACE WITH EACH OTHER. AMEN.

FOCUS ON THE BOOK OF MICAH

With what shall I come before the LORD and bow down before the exalted God? Shall I come before him with burnt offerings, with calves a year old? Will the LORD be pleased with thousands of rams, with ten thousand rivers of olive oil? Shall I offer my firstborn for my transgression, the fruit of my body for the sin of my soul? He has shown you, O mortal, what is good. And what does the LORD require of you? To act justly and to love mercy and to walk humbly with your God.

MICAH 6:6–8 NIV

When our overactive minds need worthwhile things to think about, we can focus on learning more from the book of Micah. The nations of Judah and Israel were worshipping idols instead of God and mistreating and abusing poor and needy people. Through the prophet Micah, God warned them that they would be destroyed for loving idols and cruelty.

Micah preached a message from God of both judgment and mercy, showing that God hates sin but never hates the people who sin. He wants each person to confess their sin, turn away from it, and turn back to Him for forgiveness and love. He wants us to honor Him with the ways we act fairly and kindly and humbly in our lives.

FATHER, THANK YOU FOR EACH BOOK IN THE BIBLE. HELP ME AS I LEARN FROM THE BOOK OF MICAH AND KEEP COMING BACK TO IT IN THE FUTURE. TEACH ME HOW TO APPLY ITS TRUTH TO MY LIFE AND TO SHARE IT WITH OTHERS. PLEASE DRAW ME CLOSER TO YOU THROUGH YOUR WORD. AMEN.

STRESS CAUSED BY STUFF

"Do not store up for yourselves treasures on earth, where moth and rust destroy, and where thieves break in and steal. But store up for yourselves treasures in heaven, where neither moth nor rust destroys, and where thieves do not break in or steal; for where your treasure is, there your heart will be also."

MATTHEW 6:19–21 NASB

Stuff around our homes easily piles up, and sometimes having too much stuff causes us to overthink and have anxiety. The less we have, the less we have to overthink about! We can always be looking to purge and organize the items that are collecting around our homes. Jesus taught us to be careful, because we should be storing up riches for ourselves in heaven, not on earth. We can't take one bit of stuff from earth to heaven with us, so we shouldn't get too caught up in having it here on earth.

What does it mean to gather riches in heaven? It means that God will be rewarding us with blessings that last forever in heaven based on the good things we are doing to bring glory to Him here on earth.

FATHER GOD, HELP ME TO WANT TREASURE IN HEAVEN FAR MORE THAN ANY COLLECTION OF "TREASURES" HERE ON EARTH. HELP ME TO USE WISDOM ABOUT WHAT STUFF I KEEP AND WHAT STUFF I GET RID OF. AMEN.

EVERYTHING

Do not worry. Learn to pray about everything.

PHILIPPIANS 4:6 NLV

We overthinkers can sometimes take the smallest, silliest things and mull them over endlessly. We need to remember that God cares even about those silly, small things—and we can give those thoughts and concerns over to Him for His help. He cares about the tiniest details of our lives—absolutely *everything*. It seems hard to believe, but He really does!

We can think about God's caring in terms of human relationships. We care about all the things going on in the lives of our closest family and friends because we love them so much. And God loves us so much more than even our closest family members and friends. Luke 12:7 tells us He even knows the number of hairs on our heads! So absolutely anything that is causing us to overthink, He cares and wants to hear about—the good and the bad, the big and the small.

FATHER GOD, HELP ME NOT TO THINK THAT ANYTHING IS TOO SILLY OR UNIMPORTANT TO TALK TO YOU ABOUT. THANK YOU FOR LOVING ME SO MUCH AND CARING ABOUT EVERYTHING I CARE ABOUT! AMEN.

FOCUS ON THE BOOK OF NAHUM

The Lord is good, a safe place in times of trouble. And He knows those who come to Him to be safe. But He will put an end to Nineveh by making a flood flow over it. And He will drive those who hate Him into darkness.

NAHUM 1:7–8 NLV

When our overactive minds need worthwhile things to think about, we can focus on learning more from the book of Nahum. After God sent Jonah to preach to the people of Nineveh (and Jonah finally made it there after a few days inside the big fish for disobeying at first), the people of Nineveh did repent and God had mercy on them.

But one hundred years later, they were back to doing bad things that caused all the trouble for them the first time. So God sent a message through the prophet Nahum that God was going to destroy Nineveh, and He did about fifty years after Nahum warned them. The book is a lesson that we must remember what a good, safe place God is for all who trust and follow Him. But He will destroy those who hate Him.

FATHER, THANK YOU FOR EACH BOOK IN THE BIBLE. HELP ME AS I LEARN FROM THE BOOK OF NAHUM AND KEEP COMING BACK TO IT IN THE FUTURE. TEACH ME HOW TO APPLY ITS TRUTH TO MY LIFE AND TO SHARE IT WITH OTHERS. PLEASE DRAW ME CLOSER TO YOU THROUGH YOUR WORD. AMEN.

GOD MAKES PERFECT PROMISES

"God is not human, that he should lie, not a human being, that he should change his mind. Does he speak and then not act? Does he promise and not fulfill?"

NUMBERS 23:19 NIV

People will let us down at times. But God will *never* let anyone down with a broken promise. He is the only one who can make a perfect promise. He will always keep His Word. He is not human, and He cannot lie or make mistakes. When He speaks, He is always right and true. Even the very best people who love us the most will let us down sometimes, even if they don't mean to—because they are human.

But God is above and beyond us, and we can trust Him completely. We should give Him all our worries and restless thoughts today and every day, and trust that He will give us His peace in place of them.

FATHER GOD, THANK YOU FOR BEING THE VERY BEST PROMISE KEEPER! I WANT TO KEEP READING YOUR WORD AND DRAWING CLOSER TO YOU AS MY STABILITY AND STRENGTH THROUGH EVERYTHING IN LIFE. AMEN.

FOCUS ON THE BOOK OF HABAKKUK

Even if the fig tree does not grow figs and there is no fruit on the vines, even if the olives do not grow and the fields give no food, even if there are no sheep within the fence and no cattle in the cattle-building, yet I will have joy in the Lord. I will be glad in the God Who saves me.

HABAKKUK 3:17–18 NLV

When our overactive minds need worthwhile things to think about, we can focus on learning more from the book of Habakkuk. We can all relate to asking God questions, and Habakkuk was a prophet of God who had lots of questions. He started out writing, "O Lord, how long must I call for help before You will hear?" (1:2 NLV).

We too sometimes wonder why we must wait so long on God or why He doesn't answer our prayers the way we want Him to. We can learn from Habakkuk that even though this prophet never got the exact answers he was hoping for from God, he got answers that reminded him of this: God is all-powerful and all-good, and He will work out His perfect plans in His perfect timing. We must always trust what Habakkuk learned in our own lives today.

FATHER, THANK YOU FOR EACH BOOK IN THE BIBLE. HELP ME AS I LEARN FROM THE BOOK OF HABAKKUK AND KEEP COMING BACK TO IT IN THE FUTURE. TEACH ME HOW TO APPLY ITS TRUTH TO MY LIFE AND TO SHARE IT WITH OTHERS. PLEASE DRAW ME CLOSER TO YOU THROUGH YOUR WORD. AMEN.

LIKE A BROKEN MIRROR

Now that which we see is as if we were looking in a broken mirror. But then we will see everything. Now I know only a part. But then I will know everything in a perfect way.

1 CORINTHIANS 13:12 NLV

When we're praying and asking God for answers but not understanding His ways, no matter how hard we're thinking and trying, 1 Corinthians 13:12 is important to remember. Everything in this world is broken from the perfect way God intended it—because sin entered the world when Adam and Eve chose to disobey God. And the way we see and try to understand is broken because of sin too.

But God is working out His plans, and at just the right time He will make all things new and right. Then we will see things perfectly as He does, and it will be incredible!

FATHER GOD, HELP ME TO TRUST YOU ALWAYS, EVEN WHEN I'M SO CONFUSED AND CAN'T FIGURE OUT WHAT YOU'RE DOING. PLEASE GIVE ME PEACE THAT AT JUST THE RIGHT TIME, YOU WILL FIX EVERYTHING THAT'S BROKEN. ONE DAY YOU WILL LET ME SEE THE WAY YOU DO, AND I WON'T EVER HAVE TO OVERTHINK ANYTHING AGAIN! AMEN.

FOCUS ON THE BOOK OF ZEPHANIAH

On that day the announcement to Jerusalem will be, "Cheer up, Zion! Don't be afraid! For the LORD your God is living among you. He is a mighty savior. He will take delight in you with gladness. With his love, he will calm all your fears. He will rejoice over you with joyful songs."

ZEPHANIAH 3:16–17 NLT

When our overactive minds need worthwhile things to think about, we can focus on learning more from the book of Zephaniah. The prophet Zephaniah preached a sobering message from God in the first chapter about awful suffering and judgment for the nation of Judah and all nations who turn away from God. Then he begged the people to turn to God before it was too late. And in the last chapter, he preached that despite all the bad things that will happen to those who reject God, there is great hope in God's promises for all who love and trust and obey Him.

FATHER, THANK YOU FOR THE BOOK OF ZEPHANIAH. HELP ME AS I READ IT AND KEEP COMING BACK TO IT IN THE FUTURE. TEACH ME WHAT YOU WANT ME TO LEARN FROM IT TO APPLY TO MY LIFE AND SHARE WITH OTHERS. AMEN.

NEVER ALONE

At my first defense no one came to stand by me, but all deserted me. May it not be charged against them! But the Lord stood by me and strengthened me, so that through me the message might be fully proclaimed and all the Gentiles might hear it. So I was rescued from the lion's mouth. The Lord will rescue me from every evil deed and bring me safely into his heavenly kingdom. To him be the glory forever and ever. Amen.

2 TIMOTHY 4:16–18 ESV

Sometimes we overthink with fears about being alone or abandoned. In those times, we can read and remember this account from the apostle Paul. Even with no one else there to help, God Himself was with Paul and protected him and gave him power. And Paul trusted that God would thwart every evil plan that people might have against him. Paul also knew that no matter what happened on earth, God would someday bring him into heaven forever.

FATHER GOD, THANK YOU FOR YOUR PROTECTION. I TRUST THAT NO MATTER WHAT HAPPENS HERE IN THIS WORLD, I AM NEVER ALONE, FOR YOU WILL NEVER ABANDON ME. YOU WILL ULTIMATELY ALWAYS KEEP ME SAFE, BECAUSE SOMEDAY YOU ARE GOING TO BRING ME INTO PERFECT PARADISE IN HEAVEN WITH YOU! AMEN.

FOCUS ON THE BOOK OF HAGGAI

"'Be strong, all you people of the land,' declares the LORD, 'and work. For I am with you,' declares the LORD Almighty. 'This is what I covenanted with you when you came out of Egypt. And my Spirit remains among you. Do not fear.'"

HAGGAI 2:4–5 NIV

When our overactive minds need worthwhile things to think about, we can focus on learning more from the book of Haggai. The prophet Haggai had a message for God's people to get back to work rebuilding the temple in Jerusalem. At first they had a good plan and a good start, but then they got distracted and let the project sit for years. We all can probably relate to that kind of thing. We get excited about good things God has asked us to do, and we enjoy them for a while, and then we get off track to do our own thing instead.

The book of Haggai can be a great reminder to us to keep asking God what He wants us to do and then never give up on His good plans for us. And if we do get off track, we can turn to God for help once again.

FATHER, THANK YOU FOR EACH BOOK IN THE BIBLE. HELP ME AS I LEARN FROM THE BOOK OF HAGGAI AND KEEP COMING BACK TO IT IN THE FUTURE. TEACH ME HOW TO APPLY ITS TRUTH TO MY LIFE AND TO SHARE IT WITH OTHERS. PLEASE DRAW ME CLOSER TO YOU THROUGH YOUR WORD. AMEN.

WHAT GOD HAS PLANNED FOR US

Let us put every thing out of our lives that keeps us from doing what we should. Let us keep running in the race that God has planned for us. Let us keep looking to Jesus. Our faith comes from Him and He is the One Who makes it perfect.

HEBREWS 12:1–2 NLV

Sometimes we think too much about what we might be missing out on. There are many amazing things to do in life and people to spend time with, but we sure don't have time and energy to do all the things with all the people. It's just not possible! So we need God's help to choose the best things He has for us in the midst of the many good things. (And there are plenty of not-good things we need to stay far away from too.)

The best way for us to live is to keep looking to Jesus, keep reading His Word, keep praying to Him and asking Him to show us the race God has mapped out specifically for each of our lives.

FATHER GOD, I WANT TO KEEP LOOKING TO JESUS AND FOLLOWING HIS EXAMPLE WITHOUT WORRYING WHAT I MIGHT BE MISSING OUT ON. PLEASE KEEP SHOWING ME THE GOOD RACE YOU HAVE MAPPED OUT FOR ME, THE GOOD PLANS YOU HAVE MADE FOR ME. AMEN.

FOCUS ON THE BOOK OF ZECHARIAH

This is what the LORD Almighty says: "I will save my people from the countries of the east and the west. I will bring them back to live in Jerusalem; they will be my people, and I will be faithful and righteous to them as their God."

ZECHARIAH 8:7–8 NIV

When our overactive minds need worthwhile things to think about, we can focus on learning more from the book of Zechariah. Like Haggai, the prophet Zechariah also preached to the people of Judah to encourage them to finish the good work they had started of rebuilding the temple in Jerusalem. He told them it would one day be the home of the Messiah Himself—the Savior they were hoping for, who we know is Jesus Christ. Zechariah kept encouraging the people and told them about all the blessings that would come to the Jewish people once they had obeyed and finished their good work.

We can read Zechariah's words and let them inspire and motivate us to do the good work God has for us too. When we do, we will be blessed, and we have already been so very blessed by the gift of Jesus Christ as our Savior from sin.

FATHER, THANK YOU FOR EACH BOOK IN THE BIBLE. HELP ME AS I LEARN FROM THE BOOK OF ZECHARIAH AND KEEP COMING BACK TO IT IN THE FUTURE. TEACH ME HOW TO APPLY ITS TRUTH TO MY LIFE AND TO SHARE IT WITH OTHERS. PLEASE DRAW ME CLOSER TO YOU THROUGH YOUR WORD. AMEN.

MANAGING TIME WELL

So be careful how you live. Live as men who are wise and not foolish. Make the best use of your time. These are sinful days. Do not be foolish. Understand what the Lord wants you to do.

EPHESIANS 5:15–17 NLV

When we don't manage our time wisely, we cause ourselves all kinds of anxiety and stress. We lose sleep and time for God and good relationships with others; we beat ourselves up for the mess we've made of our schedules. And the many negative effects can keep spiraling. It's far too easy to get distracted or to be lazy about doing the good work God has for us to do.

We all need to be realistic and evaluate the things that tempt us away from doing what we need to be doing and ask God to help us have good self-discipline with those things. Then we can ask Him to show us how to live carefully and wisely, making the best use of our time and using our gifts to glorify Him in all the things He has planned for us to do.

LORD, PLEASE HELP ME TO MANAGE MY TIME WISELY TO ACCOMPLISH THE THINGS I NEED TO ACCOMPLISH AND THE GOOD THINGS YOU CREATED ME FOR SO I CAN BRING GLORY TO YOU! AMEN.

INCREASE YOUR GOOD QUALITIES

For this very reason, make every effort to add to your faith goodness; and to goodness, knowledge; and to knowledge, self-control; and to self-control, perseverance; and to perseverance, godliness; and to godliness, mutual affection; and to mutual affection, love. For if you possess these qualities in increasing measure, they will keep you from being ineffective and unproductive in your knowledge of our Lord Jesus Christ.

2 PETER 1:5–8 NIV

Sometimes we overthink because we compare our personality traits with those of others, wishing we could be more like someone else. But we just need to accept the personality type God gave us and be comfortable in it. Some of us are extroverts, and some are introverts, and some of us are somewhere in between. What matters is that we're aware of how God made us and that we ask Him to use the personality and the gifts He's given to serve Him in the ways He asks.

God can continually grow and develop us with new traits and gifts and skills according to His will—if we let Him! But to do these things well, we need to stay in constant good relationship and communication with Him. So we should never stop praying. We should never stop reading God's Word. We should never stop learning from and serving our loving Father!

FATHER GOD, HELP ME TO LEARN MORE ABOUT MYSELF AND HOW YOU DESIGNED ME AS I KEEP LEARNING FROM YOU AND STAYING CLOSE TO YOU. AMEN.

FOCUS ON THE BOOK OF MALACHI

Then those who feared the LORD spoke with each other, and the LORD listened to what they said. In his presence, a scroll of remembrance was written to record the names of those who feared him and always thought about the honor of his name. "They will be my people," says the LORD of Heaven's Armies. "On the day when I act in judgment, they will be my own special treasure. I will spare them as a father spares an obedient child. Then you will again see the difference between the righteous and the wicked, between those who serve God and those who do not."

MALACHI 3:16–18 NLT

When our overactive minds need worthwhile things to think about, we can focus on learning more from the book of Malachi, which is the last book of the Old Testament. Malachi was a prophet of God who spoke a message to help bring God's people back into close relationship with Him. God wants that for us too. He is upset when we choose sin that hurts our relationship with Him, and He wants us to confess and turn away from it so that we can be close to Him again.

FATHER, THANK YOU FOR EACH BOOK IN THE BIBLE. HELP ME AS I LEARN FROM THE BOOK OF MALACHI AND KEEP COMING BACK TO IT IN THE FUTURE. TEACH ME HOW TO APPLY ITS TRUTH TO MY LIFE AND TO SHARE IT WITH OTHERS. PLEASE DRAW ME CLOSER TO YOU THROUGH YOUR WORD. AMEN.

GOD KNOWS BEFORE YOU ASK HIM

"When you pray, do not say the same thing over and over again making long prayers like the people who do not know God. They think they are heard because their prayers are long. Do not be like them. Your Father knows what you need before you ask Him."

MATTHEW 6:7–8 NLV

If God knows what we need before we even ask Him, as Matthew 6:8 says, then we might wonder, *Why should I even pray at all? God already knows!* And the answer is this: Because God loves us *that* much! He wants a close relationship with us *that* much. He wants to hear from us even though He already knows everything about us and everything we need!

The God of the whole universe wants to be close to us, and that's beyond amazing! The fact that He already knows everything about us plus everything about *everything* is a reason to want to talk to Him all the more, never a reason to think we don't need to bother praying!

GOD, YOU ARE MY GOOD AND LOVING FATHER. YOU KNOW EVERYTHING, AND YOU ALREADY KNOW EXACTLY WHAT I NEED IN EVERY SITUATION. I AM AMAZED BY YOUR GREATNESS AND THAT YOU WANT TO BE CLOSE TO ME. THANK YOU! AMEN.

FOCUS ON THE BOOK OF MATTHEW

He said to them, "But who do you say that I am?" Simon Peter said, "You are the Christ, the Son of the living God." Jesus said to him, "Simon, son of Jonah, you are happy because you did not learn this from man. My Father in heaven has shown you this."

MATTHEW 16:15–17 NLV

When our overactive minds need worthwhile things to think about, we can focus on learning more from the book of Matthew, which is the first book of the New Testament. Four hundred years passed from the time of the last book in the Old Testament, Malachi, until the time of the book of Matthew. It's one of the four Gospels, which are books that tell about the life and ministry of Jesus Christ. He's the focus because He was and is the Messiah, which means "chosen one," whom the Jewish people were eagerly waiting for. He had been promised by the prophets of God. Jesus said, "Do not think that I have come to do away with the Law of Moses or the writings of the early preachers. I have not come to do away with them but to complete them" (Matthew 5:17 NLV).

FATHER, THANK YOU FOR EACH BOOK IN THE BIBLE. HELP ME AS I LEARN FROM MATTHEW AND KEEP COMING BACK TO IT IN THE FUTURE. TEACH ME HOW TO APPLY ITS TRUTH TO MY LIFE AND TO SHARE IT WITH OTHERS. PLEASE DRAW ME CLOSER TO YOU THROUGH YOUR WORD. AMEN.

DEEP IN CHRIST, PART 1

As you have put your trust in Christ Jesus the Lord to save you from the punishment of sin, now let Him lead you in every step. Have your roots planted deep in Christ. Grow in Him. Get your strength from Him. Let Him make you strong in the faith as you have been taught. Your life should be full of thanks to Him.

COLOSSIANS 2:6–7 NLV

We can let this scripture motivate us in our relationship with Jesus every day. The deeper our roots grow into Him, the sturdier our lives are built on Him and the stronger our faith is in Him. And with deep roots, a sturdy life, and strong faith, the better we can fight off worry and fear and overthinking. We will still stress at times, of course, but we won't be totally overwhelmed. The stronger we are in relationship with Jesus, the more we will let Him take away our anxieties as we cast them on Him as His Word instructs (1 Peter 5:7).

FATHER GOD, HELP ME TO BE LIKE THE STURDIEST, TALLEST TREE WITH ROOTS THAT ARE STRONG AND GO DEEP INTO YOU. AMEN.

DEEP IN CHRIST, PART 2

"A man went out to plant seed. As he planted the seed, some fell by the side of the road. It was walked on and birds came and ate it. Some seed fell between rocks. As soon as it started to grow, it dried up because it had no water. Some seed fell among thorns. The thorns grew and did not give the seed room to grow. Some seed fell on good ground. It grew and gave one hundred times as much grain."

LUKE 8:5–8 NLV

Jesus told this parable to help us learn even more about having good strong roots that are deep in Him. And then He explained the parable like this:

> *"The seed is the Word of God. Those by the side of the road hear the Word. Then the devil comes and takes the Word from their hearts. He does not want them to believe and be saved from the punishment of sin. Those which fell among rocks are those who when they hear the Word receive it with joy. These have no root. For awhile they believe, but when they are tempted they give up. Those which fell among thorns hear the Word but go their own way. The cares of this life let the thorns grow. A love for money lets the thorns grow also. And the fun of this life lets the thorns grow. Their grain never becomes full-grown. But those which fell on good ground have heard the Word. They keep it in a good and true heart and they keep on giving good grain." (Luke 8:11–15 NLV)*

....

....

....

....

....

....

FATHER GOD, PLEASE HELP ME TO BE THAT LAST KIND OF SEED.

FOCUS ON THE BOOK OF MARK

"Whoever wants to be a leader among you must be your servant, and whoever wants to be first among you must be the slave of everyone else. For even the Son of Man came not to be served but to serve others and to give his life as a ransom for many."

MARK 10:43–45 NLT

When our overactive minds need worthwhile things to think about, we can focus on learning more from the book of Mark. Mark wrote the shortest of the four Gospels that tell about the life and ministry of Jesus. There are similarities and differences between all four of the Gospels because they are written by four different authors with different personalities and perspectives who were writing to different audiences. But the Gospels are similar in all the ways that matter most to tell us about the teaching and miracles and death and resurrection of Jesus—and how He fulfilled what the prophets had foretold in the Old Testament.

FATHER, THANK YOU FOR EACH BOOK IN THE BIBLE. HELP ME AS I LEARN FROM MARK AND KEEP COMING BACK TO IT IN THE FUTURE. TEACH ME HOW TO APPLY ITS TRUTH TO MY LIFE AND TO SHARE IT WITH OTHERS. PLEASE DRAW ME CLOSER TO YOU THROUGH YOUR WORD. AMEN.

GOD WRECKS THE PLANS OF THE PEOPLE

The Lord brings the plans of nations to nothing. He wrecks the plans of the people. The plans of the Lord stand forever. The plans of His heart stand through the future of all people. Happy is the nation whose God is the Lord. Happy are the people He has chosen for His own.

PSALM 33:10–12 NLV

Sometimes we worry that someone might have plans to hurt us. Hopefully that's never true, but this scripture from Psalm 33 helps give us peace even if it is true. God wrecks the plans of people if He wants to. He can wreck any plan for harm that someone might have against us. And if He does allow something bad to happen to us, He has plans to make us stronger because of it and turn it into something good instead.

Romans 8:28 (NLT) promises, "God causes everything to work together for the good of those who love God and are called according to his purpose for them."

FATHER GOD, I BELIEVE YOU CAN WRECK ANY BAD PLAN OR TURN IT INTO GOOD SOMEHOW, SO I NEVER NEED TO WORRY. YOU TAKE GOOD CARE OF ME, AND YOU HAVE PERFECT PLANS FOR ME. I TRUST YOU! AMEN.

THE VOICE OF THE LORD

The voice of the LORD is over the waters; the God of glory thunders, the LORD thunders over the mighty waters. The voice of the LORD is powerful; the voice of the LORD is majestic. The voice of the LORD breaks the cedars; the LORD breaks in pieces the cedars of Lebanon. He makes Lebanon leap like a calf, Sirion like a young wild ox. The voice of the LORD strikes with flashes of lightning. The voice of the LORD shakes the desert; the LORD shakes the Desert of Kadesh. The voice of the LORD twists the oaks and strips the forests bare. And in his temple all cry, "Glory!"

PSALM 29:3–9 NIV

When we're feeling overwhelmed, we should focus on the fact that no one has power to help us with any worry or stress like God does. We can let this psalm encourage us greatly! We should read it, remember it, and trust in it—and let it grow our faith in our amazing God.

With His voice, God can say or do anything at all. No matter what is going on in the world, God is always in control, always able to use His voice to help and rescue us in the good ways He chooses.

FATHER GOD, REMIND ME OF THE POWER OF YOUR AWESOME VOICE THAT IS ABLE TO DO ANYTHING AT ALL TO HELP ME AND GIVE ME PEACE! AMEN.

FOCUS ON THE BOOK OF LUKE

Many have undertaken to draw up an account of the things that have been fulfilled among us, just as they were handed down to us by those who from the first were eyewitnesses and servants of the word. With this in mind, since I myself have carefully investigated everything from the beginning, I too decided to write an orderly account for you, most excellent Theophilus, so that you may know the certainty of the things you have been taught.

LUKE 1:1–4 NIV

When our overactive minds need worthwhile things to think about, we can focus on learning more from the book of Luke. Luke revealed how Jesus was both human like us but also fully God and totally perfect without sin. He was the only one who could pay the price of sin for us by dying on the cross. And because He took our sin on Himself, He made a way for us to be right with God.

Luke wanted to make sure that everyone reading his Gospel about Jesus, no matter who they are or where they come from, could accept Jesus Christ as Savior and have a relationship with God and eternal life in His presence.

FATHER, THANK YOU FOR EACH BOOK IN THE BIBLE. HELP ME AS I LEARN FROM LUKE AND KEEP COMING BACK TO IT IN THE FUTURE. TEACH ME HOW TO APPLY ITS TRUTH TO MY LIFE AND TO SHARE IT WITH OTHERS. PLEASE DRAW ME CLOSER TO YOU THROUGH YOUR WORD. AMEN.

DON'T LET YOUR WORDS GET OUT OF HAND

When we put bits into the mouths of horses to make them obey us, we can turn the whole animal. Or take ships as an example. Although they are so large and are driven by strong winds, they are steered by a very small rudder wherever the pilot wants to go. Likewise, the tongue is a small part of the body, but it makes great boasts. Consider what a great forest is set on fire by a small spark. The tongue also is a fire, a world of evil among the parts of the body. It corrupts the whole body, sets the whole course of one's life on fire, and is itself set on fire by hell.

JAMES 3:3–6 NIV

We overthinkers can easily let our thoughts get out of hand—and sometimes we let our spoken words get out of hand too. The Bible is clear about how powerful the words we say are, so we need to remember God's wisdom that we should be careful with them. Proverbs 21:23 (NLV) says, "He who watches over his mouth and his tongue keeps his soul from troubles." And Ephesians 4:29 (NLV) says, "Watch your talk! No bad words should be coming from your mouth. Say what is good. Your words should help others grow as Christians."

FATHER GOD, PLEASE HELP ME TO REMEMBER THAT THE WORDS I SAY MATTER, AND THEY ARE POWERFUL. PLEASE HELP ME TO USE MY WORDS WISELY. AND WHEN I MESS UP WITH MY WORDS, PLEASE HELP ME TO TAKE RESPONSIBILITY AND ASK FOR FORGIVENESS. AMEN.

FOCUS ON YOUR GIFTS

We all have different gifts that God has given to us by His loving-favor. We are to use them. If someone has the gift of preaching the Good News, he should preach. He should use the faith God has given him. If someone has the gift of helping others, then he should help. If someone has the gift of teaching, he should teach. If someone has the gift of speaking words of comfort and help, he should speak. If someone has the gift of sharing what he has, he should give from a willing heart. If someone has the gift of leading other people, he should lead them. If someone has the gift of showing kindness to others, he should be happy as he does it.

ROMANS 12:6–8 NLV

God has given all of us special gifts and talents that He wants us to use to help spread His love and bring praise to Him! When we're regularly asking God to show us His good plans and purposes for our lives and then doing those things, it's hard to have time and room in our minds for any useless thoughts and worries.

Hopefully, you already know what your gifts are, and you might discover more as the years go by and you have new life experiences. We can always pray for God to give us confidence in the gifts He has given us and ask Him for opportunities to develop them more and share them well!

FATHER GOD, PLEASE SHOW ME MY GIFTS AND HOW YOU WANT ME TO USE THEM TO POINT MORE PEOPLE TO KNOWING AND LOVING YOU! AMEN.

FOCUS ON THE BOOK OF JOHN

These are written that you may believe that Jesus is the Messiah, the Son of God, and that by believing you may have life in his name.

JOHN 20:31 NIV

When our overactive minds need worthwhile things to think about, we can focus on learning more from the book of John. It's the last of the four Gospels about the life and ministry of Jesus. The book of John doesn't give details about Jesus' life as a child, but it focuses a lot on the final days of Jesus' life on earth. Over half of the book is about the events and Jesus' teaching during His last week on earth. Some of His last earthly words to His disciples were "Do not let your heart be troubled. You have put your trust in God, put your trust in Me also. There are many rooms in My Father's house. If it were not so, I would have told you. I am going away to make a place for you. After I go and make a place for you, I will come back and take you with Me" (John 14:1–3 NLV).

FATHER, THANK YOU FOR EACH BOOK IN THE BIBLE. HELP ME AS I LEARN FROM JOHN AND KEEP COMING BACK TO IT IN THE FUTURE. TEACH ME HOW TO APPLY ITS TRUTH TO MY LIFE AND TO SHARE IT WITH OTHERS. PLEASE DRAW ME CLOSER TO YOU THROUGH YOUR WORD. AMEN.

PRAY FOR ALL THOSE IN AUTHORITY

I urge, then, first of all, that petitions, prayers, intercession and thanksgiving be made for all people—for kings and all those in authority, that we may live peaceful and quiet lives in all godliness and holiness. This is good, and pleases God our Savior, who wants all people to be saved and to come to a knowledge of the truth.

1 TIMOTHY 2:1–4 NIV

If we pay attention to news about our nation and politics and current events, we'll surely have plenty of things to overthink and fear and fret about. It's tempting to believe there's not much we can really do, but there is always something—we can pray, of course! We can pray for the leaders of our nation and their families in federal, state, and local government.

Praying for so many people might seem overwhelming, but one idea is to let the American flag be a reminder. Every time we see it, it can prompt us to pray.

FATHER GOD, PLEASE BLESS OUR NATION ACCORDING TO YOUR WILL AND GIVE US PEACE. HELP OUR LEADERS TO WANT TO ACKNOWLEDGE AND HONOR YOU. PLEASE GIVE THEM YOUR WISDOM TO GOVERN WELL. I PRAY THAT EACH OF THEM AND THEIR FAMILIES WOULD BELIEVE IN YOU AS THE ONE TRUE GOD AND SAVIOR. PLEASE PROTECT OUR NATION AND PROTECT OUR FREEDOM TO WORSHIP YOU—AND HELP US TO USE THAT FREEDOM TO SPREAD YOUR TRUTH AND LOVE. AMEN.

DON'T WORRY ABOUT THE WORLD—PRAY!

"Be still, and know that I am God. I will be exalted among the nations, I will be exalted in the earth!" The Lord *of hosts is with us; the God of Jacob is our fortress.*

Psalm 46:10–11 esv

As we stay aware of current events, we can use our thoughts wisely instead of fretting. We can pray specifically for each state in our nation. And we shouldn't just stop there. God loves everyone everywhere in the whole world, not just our nation. Imagine if all believers had a prayer globe for a visual reminder and started praying regularly for every person in every country and for all nations to honor the one true God and do His will according to His Word. How amazing if we all spent time praying for the whole world, which is a far better use of time than worrying about what's going on!

FATHER GOD, YOU LOVE EVERY PERSON OF EVERY NATION, AND YOU WANT THEM TO HONOR YOU AND TRUST JESUS AS SAVIOR. YOU WANT TO GIVE THEM ETERNAL LIFE. YOU ARE SUCH A GOOD AND LOVING HEAVENLY FATHER. HELP ME TO REMEMBER TO PRAY FOR ALL PEOPLE EVERYWHERE! AMEN.

FOCUS ON THE BOOK OF ACTS

He said to them: "It is not for you to know the times or dates the Father has set by his own authority. But you will receive power when the Holy Spirit comes on you; and you will be my witnesses in Jerusalem, and in all Judea and Samaria, and to the ends of the earth."

ACTS 1:7–8 NIV

When our overactive minds need worthwhile things to think about, we can focus on learning more from the book of Acts. At the end of the Gospels, Jesus had risen from the dead and appeared to various people to prove that He was alive. The book of Acts picks up right where the Gospel of Luke left off (and is written by the same doctor, Luke), and soon Jesus went up to heaven to be with God the Father.

But Jesus didn't want to leave people alone without Him on earth. He promised to send the Holy Spirit in His place. The book of Acts tells about how that promise came true and how the group of believers in Jesus, called "the church," started out with 120 people and then grew and grew as those believers kept spreading the good news about our Savior Jesus and more and more people believed in Him.

FATHER, THANK YOU FOR EACH BOOK IN THE BIBLE. HELP ME AS I LEARN FROM ACTS AND KEEP COMING BACK TO IT IN THE FUTURE. TEACH ME HOW TO APPLY ITS TRUTH TO MY LIFE AND TO SHARE IT WITH OTHERS. PLEASE DRAW ME CLOSER TO YOU THROUGH YOUR WORD. AMEN.

GOD IS ALWAYS THE SAME

Jesus Christ is the same yesterday and today and forever.

HEBREWS 13:8 ESV

Big change in our lives, or even lots of little changes all at once, can cause worry and stress and extreme overthinking. What ways have you experienced stress because of changes? What were your thoughts and emotions and prayers like during that time?

Nothing in life will always stay the same, and that's why we can be so thankful that God gave us Jesus, who is always dependable and always the same—yesterday, today, and forever! Psalm 102:25–27 (NLV) says of God, "You made the earth in the beginning. You made the heavens with Your hands. They will be destroyed but You will always live. They will all become old as clothing becomes old. You will change them like a coat. And they will be changed, but You are always the same. Your years will never end."

God is never going to change or let us down. So we can lean on Him and ask Him to hold us steady when life seems to swirl around us with new circumstances. We can talk to Him about every joy and sorrow and stress.

FATHER GOD, THANK YOU FOR NEVER CHANGING OR FAILING ME THROUGH ALL OF LIFE'S UPS AND DOWNS! AMEN.

THE SUN STOOD STILL AND THE MOON STOPPED

At that time Joshua spoke to the Lord in the day when the Lord gave the Amorites over to the sons of Israel, and he said in the sight of Israel, "Sun, stand still at Gibeon, and moon, in the Valley of Aijalon." And the sun stood still, and the moon stopped, until the nation took vengeance on their enemies. Is this not written in the Book of Jashar? The sun stopped in the midst of heaven and did not hurry to set for about a whole day. There has been no day like it before or since, when the Lord heeded the voice of a man, for the Lord fought for Israel.

Joshua 10:12–14 ESV

The story of God causing the sun and moon to stand still is a remarkable story to remember when we're praying for God to help ease our minds when they're full of too many thoughts and worries. Joshua prayed for the sun and moon to stand still to give extra daylight in order for God's people to win the war against their enemies, the Amorites. And God answered in a way He had never done before and has never done again.

Clearly, God can do *absolutely anything*, so He can certainly calm our anxiety. He is able to help us in extraordinary ways with every one of our needs, as well as the needs of our families and friends!

FATHER GOD, PLEASE REMIND ME CONSTANTLY OF YOUR ALL-POWERFUL WAYS! NO PROBLEM OR WORRY OR FEAR I HAVE IS EVER TOO BIG FOR YOU! YOU ARE ALMIGHTY AND AMAZING AND WORTHY OF ALL MY PRAISE! AMEN.

FOCUS ON THE BOOK OF ROMANS

Jesus died for our sins. He was raised from the dead to make us right with God. Now that we have been made right with God by putting our trust in Him, we have peace with Him. It is because of what our Lord Jesus Christ did for us.

ROMANS 4:25–5:1 NLV

When our overactive minds need worthwhile things to think about, we can focus on learning more from the book of Romans. It's the first in a series of books that are kind of like reading someone else's mail. Obviously, we shouldn't do that without permission, but we absolutely have permission to read the letters (or epistles, as they're sometimes called) included in the Bible. God wants you to read and learn from them.

The book of Romans was a letter written by the apostle Paul. The story of how his life was totally transformed by Jesus is back in Acts. Paul wrote to the group of believers in the city of Rome to explain to them fully what it means to have salvation by trusting in Jesus as the sacrifice for sin.

FATHER, THANK YOU FOR EACH BOOK IN THE BIBLE. HELP ME AS I LEARN FROM ROMANS AND KEEP COMING BACK TO IT IN THE FUTURE. TEACH ME HOW TO APPLY ITS TRUTH TO MY LIFE AND TO SHARE IT WITH OTHERS. PLEASE DRAW ME CLOSER TO YOU THROUGH YOUR WORD. AMEN.

SALT OF THE EARTH, LIGHT OF THE WORLD

"You are the salt of the earth. But if the salt loses its saltiness, how can it be made salty again? . . . You are the light of the world. A town built on a hill cannot be hidden. Neither do people light a lamp and put it under a bowl. Instead they put it on its stand, and it gives light to everyone in the house. In the same way, let your light shine before others, that they may see your good deeds and glorify your Father in heaven."

MATTHEW 5:13–16 NIV

Sometimes we think too hard about sharing our faith, and we let worry and anxiety stop us from doing so. We might feel that it's best just to stay mostly quiet about it. But that's exactly what our enemy Satan wants. Jesus said we should want to be like salt and light. Salt helps food taste its best, and we should want to bring out the best in others and help show them life at its best.

Life at its best is a life that believes in and follows Jesus. Jesus also wants us to be the light of the world. If we hide our light, we can't help others see the way to Jesus. But if we shine our light, giving Him honor through every good thing we do, we help others honor Him too.

DEAR JESUS, I DON'T WANT TO WORRY ABOUT SHARING MY FAITH. I WANT TO SHINE LIKE YOU'VE ASKED ME TO AND REACH OUT TO OTHERS AND BE SALT AND LIGHT TO THEM, HELPING THEM KNOW AND LOVE YOU TOO! AMEN.

HELP IS FROM THE LORD

I lift up my eyes to the mountains—where does my help come from? My help comes from the LORD, the Maker of heaven and earth. He will not let your foot slip—he who watches over you will not slumber; indeed, he who watches over Israel will neither slumber nor sleep. The LORD watches over you—the LORD is your shade at your right hand; the sun will not harm you by day, nor the moon by night. The LORD will keep you from all harm—he will watch over your life; the LORD will watch over your coming and going both now and forevermore.

PSALM 121 NIV

Every bit of help we get for anything ultimately comes from God. He is the one watching over us at all times and providing the people and things and opportunities we need when we need them. We can praise and thank Him every time we ask for help and receive it—and for all the ways we are helped without ever even having to ask!

FATHER GOD, EVERYTHING GOOD COMES FROM YOU! I CAN NEVER THANK YOU ENOUGH FOR THE COUNTLESS WAYS YOU HELP ME EVERY DAY. AMEN.

FOCUS ON THE BOOKS OF 1 AND 2 CORINTHIANS

This letter is from Paul. I have been chosen by God to be a missionary of Jesus Christ. Sosthenes, a Christian brother, writes also. I write to God's church in the city of Corinth. I write to those who belong to Christ Jesus and to those who are set apart by Him and made holy. I write to all the Christians everywhere who call on the name of Jesus Christ. He is our Lord and their Lord also. May you have loving-favor and peace from God our Father and from the Lord Jesus Christ.

1 Corinthians 1:1–3 nlv

When our overactive minds need worthwhile things to think about, we can focus on learning more from the books of 1 and 2 Corinthians. They are more letters from the apostle Paul, this time to a church in the city of Corinth in Greece. Paul had heard that the Christians in the Corinthian church were not living as they should or treating each other as well as they should. His letters were meant to correct their wrongs and encourage them to do right, according to God's good ways.

We can read these letters and let them help us correct our wrongs and do what is right according to God's good ways too.

....

....

....

....

....

....

FATHER, THANK YOU FOR EACH BOOK IN THE BIBLE. HELP ME AS I LEARN FROM 1 AND 2 CORINTHIANS AND KEEP COMING BACK TO THEM IN THE FUTURE. TEACH ME HOW TO APPLY THEIR TRUTH TO MY LIFE AND TO SHARE IT WITH OTHERS. PLEASE DRAW ME CLOSER TO YOU THROUGH YOUR WORD. AMEN.

TRUE EQUALITY

You are now children of God because you have put your trust in Christ Jesus. All of you who have been baptized to show you belong to Christ have become like Christ. God does not see you as a Jew or as a Greek. He does not see you as a servant or as a person free to work. He does not see you as a man or as a woman. You are all one in Christ.

GALATIANS 3:26–28 NLV

We hear the word *equality* a lot these days, and it's hard not to overthink it and it's stressful to figure out who to listen to about it. We need wisdom about who alone gives real equality—Jesus!

Because of sin in the world, people will never get equality exactly right. There will always be bad people trying to say some groups of people are better than others. But we don't ever have to listen to or join them. In God's eyes, because of Jesus, every single person is the same in value. We all matter so much to God that He sent Jesus to die to save us from our sins.

And when anyone trusts in Jesus, they become a child of the one true God, the King of all kings. That makes believers equally royal, and we should want to share that awesome truth with everyone we can!

FATHER GOD, YOU OFFER THE ONLY TRUE EQUALITY THROUGH JESUS. THANK YOU THAT ANYONE CAN BE YOUR CHILD BY TRUSTING THAT ONLY JESUS SAVES. HELP ME TO SHARE YOUR LOVE AND TRUTH. AMEN.

MORNING PRAYERS

Hear my words, O Lord. Think about my crying. Listen to my cry for help, my King and my God. For I pray to you. In the morning, O Lord, You will hear my voice. In the morning I will lay my prayers before You and will look up.

PSALM 5:1–3 NLV

Our busy minds can keep us up late at night or they can wake us early in the morning. Being an overthinker can be exhausting! Whatever our tendencies, whether we're night owls or early birds, it's best to start our days with prayer.

Before we even get out of bed, we can ask God to help us control our minds and focus well on how we can best serve and please Him today. We can ask Him to bless us and keep us close to Him. We can ask Him to help us depend completely on His strength and power. We can ask for His wisdom to teach and guide us and for direction to show us how to share His love and truth with others.

FATHER GOD, PLEASE HELP MY BUSY THOUGHTS TO FIRST GO TO YOU WHEN I WAKE UP! SHOW ME HOW TO SERVE YOU EACH DAY. PLEASE BLESS ME AND HELP ME TO STAY CLOSE TO YOU. PLEASE GIVE ME YOUR STRENGTH AND POWER THROUGH YOUR HOLY SPIRIT. PLEASE GIVE ME WISDOM AND TEACH ME AND GUIDE ME—AND HELP ME TO SHARE YOUR TRUTH AND LOVE WITH THOSE AROUND ME. AMEN.

FOCUS ON THE BOOK OF GALATIANS

Christ made us free. Stay that way. Do not get chained all over again in the Law and its kind of religious worship.

GALATIANS 5:1 NLV

When our overactive minds need worthwhile things to think about, we can focus on learning more from the book of Galatians. Paul wrote this letter to the churches in Galatia to correct them because many people there were listening to some false teachers who taught that salvation in Jesus meant to believe in Him plus following lots of Jewish customs and rules. But salvation in Jesus comes simply from believing in Him and accepting His gift of grace to pay for sin.

We find tremendous freedom and relief in trusting that truth and realizing that it's Jesus' work when He died on the cross that saves us and gives us eternal life, not any work we do or rules we follow. We should want to share that truth with *all* people so that they can have everlasting freedom in Jesus too.

FATHER, THANK YOU FOR EACH BOOK IN THE BIBLE. HELP ME AS I LEARN FROM GALATIANS AND KEEP COMING BACK TO IT IN THE FUTURE. TEACH ME HOW TO APPLY ITS TRUTH TO MY LIFE AND TO SHARE IT WITH OTHERS. PLEASE DRAW ME CLOSER TO YOU THROUGH YOUR WORD. AMEN.

POWER TO HEAL

[Jesus] touched her hand, and the fever left her, and she rose and began to serve him. That evening they brought to him many who were oppressed by demons, and he cast out the spirits with a word and healed all who were sick.

MATTHEW 8:15–16 ESV

When our minds are consumed with worry over an illness in ourselves or a loved one, we must remember God's amazing power to heal! When Jesus was on earth, He showed that He truly was God with His divine ability to heal people of sickness and demons. Jesus still has the power to heal now, and we can pray and ask God for healing for people who need it. But we also need wisdom about this.

God heals people on a case-by-case basis, so it isn't up to us to tell God how to heal someone. He may heal instantaneously, through natural means, or through medical care. He may even choose to take a suffering person home to heaven to be with Him, where they will be well forever. So even more important than praying for healing on earth is to pray that the people who need it know Jesus as Savior so that they can have eternal life. As we do pray for healing, we can do it with great faith, certain that God is absolutely able and that He always does what is right and good.

DEAR JESUS, YOU HAVE THE POWER TO HEAL AND PERFORM ANY MIRACLE, INCLUDING HEALING FROM ANY KIND OF SICKNESS! PLEASE GIVE ME WISDOM AS I PRAY FOR YOUR WILL TO BE DONE. AMEN.

LET US NOT GROW WEARY OF DOING GOOD

Let us not grow weary of doing good, for in due season we will reap, if we do not give up. So then, as we have opportunity, let us do good to everyone, and especially to those who are of the household of faith.

GALATIANS 6:9–10 ESV

Overthinking can tire us out. And if we're not careful, it is really easy to get tired of doing good and making the right choices to obey God. Our enemy wants us to think it's too hard, too exhausting, to follow Jesus. Making bad choices and acting selfishly seems the easy, comfortable way a lot of the time. And sometimes it is a lot easier at first, but in the long run it will cause us all kinds of anxiety and consequences.

God's ways are always best for us. And He will help us not to get worn out if we ask Him. He can give us everything we need for doing the good things He has planned for us.

FATHER GOD, HELP ME TO FIND ALL STRENGTH AND ENDURANCE AND EVERYTHING I NEED IN YOU SO THAT I NEVER TIRE OF DOING GOOD AND NEVER GIVE UP. AMEN.

FOCUS ON THE BOOK OF EPHESIANS

Even before he made the world, God loved us and chose us in Christ to be holy and without fault in his eyes. God decided in advance to adopt us into his own family by bringing us to himself through Jesus Christ. This is what he wanted to do, and it gave him great pleasure. So we praise God for the glorious grace he has poured out on us who belong to his dear Son. He is so rich in kindness and grace that he purchased our freedom with the blood of his Son and forgave our sins. He has showered his kindness on us, along with all wisdom and understanding.

EPHESIANS 1:4–8 NLT

When our overactive minds need worthwhile things to think about, we can focus on learning more from the book of Ephesians. It's Paul's letter to the church in the city of Ephesus, and it's all about *encouragement*. There is no specific wrong that Paul is wanting to correct in the church at Ephesus; he simply wants to encourage the believers there in their faith and identity in Jesus and show them how that faith and identity should play out in their daily lives. We can read Ephesians for great encouragement in our own lives today too.

FATHER, THANK YOU FOR EACH BOOK IN THE BIBLE. HELP ME AS I LEARN FROM EPHESIANS AND KEEP COMING BACK TO IT IN THE FUTURE. TEACH ME HOW TO APPLY ITS TRUTH TO MY LIFE AND TO SHARE IT WITH OTHERS. PLEASE DRAW ME CLOSER TO YOU THROUGH YOUR WORD. AMEN.

FOCUS ON THE BOOK OF PHILIPPIANS

Be full of joy always because you belong to the Lord. Again I say, be full of joy!

PHILIPPIANS 4:4 NLV

When our overactive minds need worthwhile things to think about, we can focus on learning more from the book of Philippians. It's another book of the Bible to go to for great encouragement. Paul wrote this letter to the church in the city of Philippi, and it's known as his letter of joy. The word *joy* is used over and over throughout the letter. The believers there had encouraged Paul and given him great joy, and he wanted to write to show them how much he appreciated them. He also wanted to remind them that real joy always depends on Jesus.

As believers in Jesus, we can have joy even during times of suffering because we have faith and hope in Him to make us strong in the middle of it, help us through it, and rescue us from it. Paul said, "I can do all things because Christ gives me the strength" (Philippians 4:13 NLV). And we can say that too!

FATHER, THANK YOU FOR EACH BOOK IN THE BIBLE. HELP ME AS I LEARN FROM PHILIPPIANS AND KEEP COMING BACK TO IT IN THE FUTURE. TEACH ME HOW TO APPLY ITS TRUTH TO MY LIFE AND TO SHARE IT WITH OTHERS. PLEASE DRAW ME CLOSER TO YOU THROUGH YOUR WORD. AMEN.

EVEN IF THE MOUNTAINS CRUMBLE INTO THE SEA

God is our refuge and strength, always ready to help in times of trouble. So we will not fear when earthquakes come and the mountains crumble into the sea. Let the oceans roar and foam. Let the mountains tremble as the waters surge! A river brings joy to the city of our God, the sacred home of the Most High. God dwells in that city; it cannot be destroyed. From the very break of day, God will protect it. The nations are in chaos, and their kingdoms crumble! God's voice thunders, and the earth melts! The Lord *of Heaven's Armies is here among us; the God of Israel is our fortress.*

PSALM 46:1–7 NLT

Our imaginations can run completely wild. We can get really good at catastrophic thinking. So we need to memorize and recite and repeat this psalm during any type of worry or fear. We are always safe when we are in God's care. He is our refuge and our strength in times of trouble—even the worst kind of trouble we can possibly imagine.

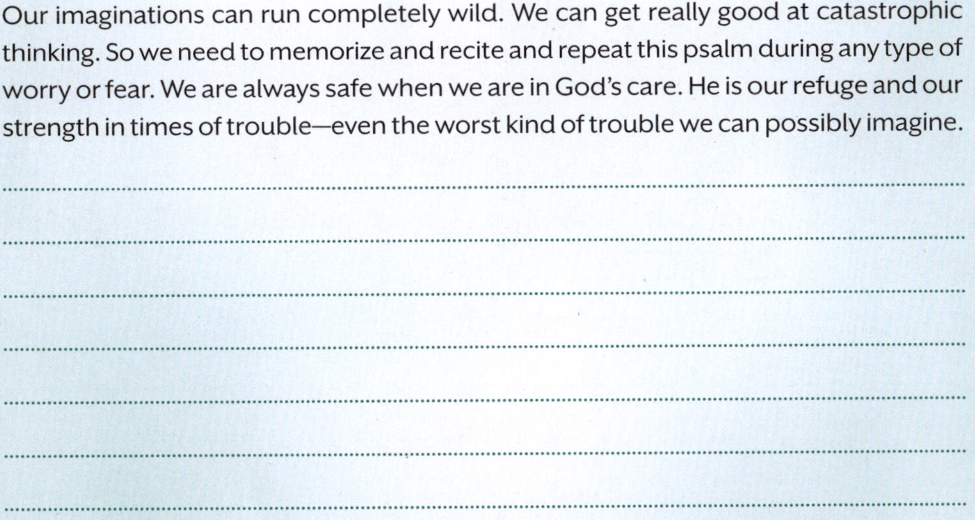

FATHER GOD, I HAVE NOTHING TO FEAR BECAUSE YOU KEEP ME SAFE. PLEASE HELP ME TO REMEMBER THAT YOU ARE MY FORTRESS, MY REFUGE IN ANY AND EVERY LIFE EVENT. THANK YOU FOR YOUR STRENGTH AND CARE AND PROTECTION. AMEN.

BUILDING UP

But you, beloved, building yourselves up in your most holy faith and praying in the Holy Spirit, keep yourselves in the love of God, waiting for the mercy of our Lord Jesus Christ that leads to eternal life.

JUDE 20–21 ESV

We all know that no building can stand for long unless it has a strong foundation. And likewise, our lives need a strong foundation of faith in the one true God or we can easily be overwhelmed and destroyed by stress and anxiety.

Prayer is a major source of support as we build lives of faith with strong foundations as followers of Jesus. Spending time in God's Word, learning at a Bible-teaching church, serving God by serving others, and having fellowship with other Christians are all major sources of strength and support too. We need to regularly evaluate and prioritize, asking ourselves: *How am I doing in all these things these days?*

FATHER GOD, I WANT TO BE BUILT UP STRONG IN MY FAITH IN YOU. HELP ME TO PRAY AND LEARN AND SERVE YOU ALL OF MY DAYS! AMEN.

FOCUS ON THE BOOK OF COLOSSIANS

You were his enemies, separated from him by your evil thoughts and actions. Yet now he has reconciled you to himself through the death of Christ in his physical body. As a result, he has brought you into his own presence, and you are holy and blameless as you stand before him without a single fault. But you must continue to believe this truth and stand firmly in it. Don't drift away from the assurance you received when you heard the Good News. The Good News has been preached all over the world, and I, Paul, have been appointed as God's servant to proclaim it.

COLOSSIANS 1:21–23 NLT

When our overactive minds need worthwhile things to think about, we can focus on learning more from the book of Colossians. Paul wrote this letter to the church in the city of Colossae because he had heard they were listening to false teaching that incorporated ideas from other religions into the Christian faith and the good news of Jesus. Throughout our whole lives, we will hear about false teaching like this too, and so it's good for us to come back to read Colossians again and again to stay true to what God's Word wants us to know about Jesus and how to follow Him.

FATHER, THANK YOU FOR EACH BOOK IN THE BIBLE. HELP ME AS I LEARN FROM COLOSSIANS AND KEEP COMING BACK TO IT IN THE FUTURE. TEACH ME HOW TO APPLY ITS TRUTH TO MY LIFE AND TO SHARE IT WITH OTHERS. PLEASE DRAW ME CLOSER TO YOU THROUGH YOUR WORD. AMEN.

OVER IT

But when I am afraid, I will put my trust in you. I praise God for what he has promised. I trust in God, so why should I be afraid? What can mere mortals do to me?

PSALM 56:3–4 NLT

Thinking back to a fear or worry we triumphed over in the past can be very helpful. We can ask ourselves, *What happened? How did God help me get over it? Who were the people and the things and ways He provided to help me get over it?* It's good to take time every once in a while to think about things we used to be worried about and afraid of that now seem like no big deal. It helps us realize that whatever is making us overthink and feel anxious today will likely one day be no big deal either.

God never leaves us alone. He is with us in the middle of our worries, and we can call out for His help at any time. He will guide us through to the other side where we can look back with relief and say, "Wow! Thanks, God! We conquered that together, and now I'm not worried about it anymore!"

FATHER GOD, I REMEMBER ALL THE WAYS YOU HAVE HELPED ME CONQUER WORRIES AND FEARS IN THE PAST, AND I AM TRUSTING THAT YOU WILL CONTINUE TO NOW AND IN THE FUTURE. AMEN.

PRAY BIG!

Oh, how great are God's riches and wisdom and knowledge! How impossible it is for us to understand his decisions and his ways! For who can know the Lord's thoughts? Who knows enough to give him advice? And who has given him so much that he needs to pay it back? For everything comes from him and exists by his power and is intended for his glory. All glory to him forever! Amen.

ROMANS 11:33–36 NLT

God's riches and power and thoughts and ways are far above and beyond anything we can possibly imagine. So, we can remember to pray big, telling God that we know that nothing is impossible for Him and that His power keeps all things together; yet we should also pray humbly, asking according to His will. And whether His answers to our prayers are what we hoped for or not, we should still want to draw closer to Him and strengthen our faith in Him.

FATHER GOD, REMIND ME TO FOCUS ON HOW AWESOME YOU ARE, ESPECIALLY WHEN I'M FEELING WORRIED. MY MIND CAN'T FULLY UNDERSTAND YOU, BUT I WANT TO GROW CLOSER TO YOU AND HONOR YOU. PLEASE STRENGTHEN MY FAITH IN YOU AND MY RELATIONSHIP WITH YOU EVERY DAY OF MY LIFE. AMEN.

FOCUS ON THE BOOKS OF 1 AND 2 THESSALONIANS

The Lord is faithful. He will give you strength and keep you safe from the devil. We have faith in the Lord for you. We believe you are doing and will keep on doing the things we told you. May the Lord lead your hearts into the love of God. May He help you as you wait for Christ.

2 THESSALONIANS 3:3–5 NLV

When our overactive minds need worthwhile things to think about, we can focus on learning more from the books of 1 and 2 Thessalonians. Paul wrote to the Christians in the city of Thessalonica to encourage them and teach them more about living for God and growing in their faith. He also encouraged them about hope in Jesus' return to gather all believers to be with Him forever in heaven. Then he wrote a second letter to clear up confusion about Jesus' return and to encourage the believers in Thessalonica to keep working while waiting on Jesus and not to get tired of doing what is right.

As we wait for Jesus today, we must also keep doing the good work God has planned for us.

FATHER, THANK YOU FOR EACH BOOK IN THE BIBLE. HELP ME AS I LEARN FROM 1 AND 2 THESSALONIANS AND KEEP COMING BACK TO THEM IN THE FUTURE. TEACH ME HOW TO APPLY THEIR TRUTH TO MY LIFE AND TO SHARE IT WITH OTHERS. PLEASE DRAW ME CLOSER TO YOU THROUGH YOUR WORD. AMEN.

SOMETIMES IT'S GOOD TO FEEL BAD

Cling to your faith in Christ, and keep your conscience clear. For some people have deliberately violated their consciences; as a result, their faith has been shipwrecked.

1 TIMOTHY 1:19 NLT

Sometimes overthinking and anxiety fill us because we're holding on to sin. We can't be free of our anxiety until we confess to God and ask for forgiveness from those we've hurt. Because He loves us so much, God sometimes purposefully makes us feel restless inside through His Holy Spirit. That feeling serving as a reminder to confess sin is a whole lot better than letting lies and sin get bigger and bigger in our lives.

Usually, as soon as we admit and confess the sin and ask for forgiveness, the anxiety it was causing is gone. Therefore we should welcome the kind of anxiety that motivates us to admit our sins and make them right.

FATHER GOD, PLEASE HELP ME TO CHOOSE TO LIVE BY YOUR WORD. BUT WHEN I DO MESS UP, I WANT TO FEEL BAD ABOUT SINNING AND CHOOSING TO HOLD ON TO IT. HELP ME TO ADMIT AND CONFESS MY SINS AND ASK FOR FORGIVENESS QUICKLY EVERY TIME. THANK YOU FOR YOUR GRACE! AMEN.

WE DON'T HAVE TO MULL IT OVER

If we claim we have no sin, we are only fooling ourselves and not living in the truth. But if we confess our sins to him, he is faithful and just to forgive us our sins and to cleanse us from all wickedness.

1 JOHN 1:8–9 NLT

Even after we have confessed our sin and asked for forgiveness from God and those we've hurt, we sometimes keep mulling it over and feeling awful for what we did wrong. But God promises time and again in His Word that we shouldn't. He removes our sins as far as the east is from the west (Psalm 103:11–12)! If God doesn't hold our sin against us, why on earth should we?

Our enemy Satan wants us to focus on our mistakes and beat ourselves up so that we feel endlessly defeated and useless. Therefore, we must pray against the enemy and believe in the power of Jesus to forgive us and totally remove our sins from us.

FATHER GOD, WHEN I CONFESS MY SIN, YOU WANT ME TO FEEL RELIEVED, FORGIVEN, AND FREE FROM IT! I TRUST THAT YOU LOVE AND FORGIVE PERFECTLY AND COMPLETELY! AMEN.

FOCUS ON THE BOOKS OF 1 AND 2 TIMOTHY

This letter is from Paul, a missionary of Jesus Christ. I am sent by God, the One Who saves, and by our Lord Jesus Christ Who is our hope. I write to you, Timothy. You are my son in the Christian faith. May God the Father and Jesus Christ our Lord give you His loving-favor and loving-kindness and peace.

1 TIMOTHY 1:1–2 NLV

When our overactive minds need worthwhile things to think about, we can focus on learning more from the books of 1 and 2 Timothy. In these books, Paul wrote to Timothy, a younger friend and pastor of a church in the city of Ephesus, to encourage him and teach him how to lead his church well, including instructions about how to care for widows and a warning to avoid the love of money. Paul wrote another letter to Timothy sharing final words of encouragement and motivation that can encourage and motivate us in our faith today too.

FATHER, THANK YOU FOR EACH BOOK IN THE BIBLE. HELP ME AS I LEARN FROM 1 AND 2 TIMOTHY AND KEEP COMING BACK TO THEM IN THE FUTURE. TEACH ME HOW TO APPLY THEIR TRUTH TO MY LIFE AND TO SHARE IT WITH OTHERS. PLEASE DRAW ME CLOSER TO YOU THROUGH YOUR WORD. AMEN.

WITH JUST A WORD

"Only speak the word, and my servant will be healed."

MATTHEW 8:8 NLV

When we pray, we need to remember the example of the army captain in the Gospel of Matthew. He had such great faith that Jesus could simply say the word and his servant would be healed that he didn't overthink anything about his request of Jesus.

> *Jesus came to the city of Capernaum. A captain of the army came to Him. He asked for help, saying, "Lord, my servant is sick in bed. He is not able to move his body. He is in much pain." Jesus said to the captain, "I will come and heal him." The captain said, "Lord, I am not good enough for You to come to my house. Only speak the word, and my servant will be healed. . . ." When Jesus heard this, He was surprised and wondered about it. He said to those who followed Him, "For sure, I tell you, I have not found so much faith in the Jewish nation. . . ." Jesus said to the captain, "Go your way. It is done for you even as you had faith to believe." The servant was healed at that time. (Matthew 8:5–8, 10, 13 NLV)*

FATHER GOD, PLEASE GROW MY FAITH IN YOU TO BE AS STRONG AND SURE AS THIS ARMY CAPTAIN'S. I BELIEVE YOU CAN JUST SAY THE WORD AND MAKE A MIRACLE HAPPEN! AMEN.

GATHER AND PRAY

"Again, truly I tell you that if two of you on earth agree about anything they ask for, it will be done for them by my Father in heaven. For where two or three gather in my name, there am I with them."

MATTHEW 18:19–20 NIV

Do you have friends or family members with whom you share needs and concerns? Do you also spend time praying about those things together? If not, it's wise to start by initiating a regular prayer time with your family. At church or work or school or your activities—or all of those—you can offer to pray for your friends and coworkers and ask them to pray for you too.

We believers all need to find efficient and effective ways and times for corporate prayer. Prayer is always powerful; and gathering to support each other and joining together in prayer brings about more of the benefits and power of prayer.

FATHER GOD, THANK YOU FOR FAMILY AND FRIENDS AND THE TIMES WHEN WE GATHER SO WE CAN ALL TALK TO YOU TOGETHER! THESE TIMES ARE ENCOURAGING, AND I WANT TO MAKE THEM A HABIT. AMEN.

FOCUS ON THE BOOK OF TITUS

In the same way, encourage the young men to live wisely. And you yourself must be an example to them by doing good works of every kind. Let everything you do reflect the integrity and seriousness of your teaching. Teach the truth so that your teaching can't be criticized. Then those who oppose us will be ashamed and have nothing bad to say about us.

TITUS 2:6–8 NLT

When our overactive minds need worthwhile things to think about, we can focus on learning more from the book of Titus. Titus was a close friend and travel companion to Paul, and Paul wrote a letter to Titus to instruct him on how to organize and lead the church and how to teach others to live for God. We can still learn much wisdom today from the lessons that were originally for Titus.

FATHER, THANK YOU FOR EACH BOOK IN THE BIBLE. HELP ME AS I LEARN FROM TITUS AND KEEP COMING BACK TO IT IN THE FUTURE. TEACH ME HOW TO APPLY ITS TRUTH TO MY LIFE AND TO SHARE IT WITH OTHERS. PLEASE DRAW ME CLOSER TO YOU THROUGH YOUR WORD. AMEN.

WHEN WE DON'T KNOW HOW TO PRAY

In the same way, the Spirit helps us in our weakness. We do not know what we ought to pray for, but the Spirit himself intercedes for us through wordless groans. And he who searches our hearts knows the mind of the Spirit, because the Spirit intercedes for God's people in accordance with the will of God.

ROMANS 8:26–27 NIV

During terrible and traumatic times for ourselves or loved ones, it can feel almost impossible to control our racing thoughts, let alone know how to pray. So we can be thankful that the Bible tells us that the Holy Spirit prays for us, taking our words and explaining them to God in exactly the best ways. And God promises to work out everything according to His will and for our good.

When we're feeling unsure of how to pray, we can tell God exactly that and then keep on praying. We can ask the Holy Spirit to take our words and make them the best they can be before God, who loves us dearly and will work out His plans perfectly.

FATHER GOD, I'M NOT ALWAYS SURE WHAT TO SAY TO YOU, BUT I NEVER WANT TO STOP TALKING TO YOU IN PRAYER. THANK YOU FOR THE HOLY SPIRIT, WHO IS INTERCEDING FOR ME. AMEN.

FOCUS ON REAL RICHES

"A rich man had a fertile farm that produced fine crops. He said to himself, 'What should I do? I don't have room for all my crops.' Then he said, 'I know! I'll tear down my barns and build bigger ones. Then I'll have room enough to store all my wheat and other goods. And I'll sit back and say to myself, "My friend, you have enough stored away for years to come. Now take it easy! Eat, drink, and be merry!"' But God said to him, 'You fool! You will die this very night. Then who will get everything you worked for?' Yes, a person is a fool to store up earthly wealth but not have a rich relationship with God."

LUKE 12:16–21 NLT

Jesus shared this parable to teach us that when we have a lot, we shouldn't overthink about saving it up. We should be willing to share generously with others.

No person has any idea exactly how long he or she will live on the earth. It's far better to be generous than to selfishly store up everything we have. Our goal should be to have real riches that come from a close relationship with God, not the riches and fleeting stuff of this world.

FATHER GOD, PLEASE HELP ME NOT TO FOCUS ON STORING UP MONEY AND POSSESSIONS. PLEASE GIVE ME A HEART THAT LOVES TO SHARE WHAT I HAVE, SINCE IT IS ALL A GIFT FROM YOU! HELP ME TO FOCUS ON REAL RICHES THAT COME FROM DRAWING CLOSER AND CLOSER IN RELATIONSHIP WITH YOU. AMEN.

FOCUS ON THE BOOK OF PHILEMON

It seems you lost Onesimus for a little while so that you could have him back forever. He is no longer like a slave to you. He is more than a slave, for he is a beloved brother, especially to me. Now he will mean much more to you, both as a man and as a brother in the Lord.

PHILEMON 15–16 NLT

When our overactive minds need worthwhile things to think about, we can focus on learning more from the book of Philemon. This biblical letter is all about a slave named Onesimus who ran away from his owner, Philemon. Onesimus met Paul in Rome and became a Christian. So Paul decided to write to Philemon to ask him to please forgive Onesimus and view him not as a slave but as a fellow believer and brother in Jesus Christ.

The book of Philemon teaches and reminds us to treat all people as equally loved and respected, especially believers in Jesus, who are members of God's family.

FATHER, THANK YOU FOR EACH BOOK IN THE BIBLE. HELP ME AS I LEARN FROM PHILEMON AND KEEP COMING BACK TO IT IN THE FUTURE. TEACH ME HOW TO APPLY ITS TRUTH TO MY LIFE AND TO SHARE IT WITH OTHERS. PLEASE DRAW ME CLOSER TO YOU THROUGH YOUR WORD. AMEN.

FOCUS ON GRATITUDE

As [Jesus] entered a village, he was met by ten lepers, who stood at a distance and lifted up their voices, saying, "Jesus, Master, have mercy on us." When he saw them he said to them, "Go and show yourselves to the priests." And as they went they were cleansed. Then one of them, when he saw that he was healed, turned back, praising God with a loud voice; and he fell on his face at Jesus' feet, giving him thanks. Now he was a Samaritan. Then Jesus answered, "Were not ten cleansed? Where are the nine? Was no one found to return and give praise to God except this foreigner?" And he said to him, "Rise and go your way; your faith has made you well."

LUKE 17:12–19 ESV

Focusing on gratitude is a great way to soothe anxiety and calm our busy minds. But sometimes we just forget to be grateful. This account in Luke 17 reminds us of how easy it is to forget to say thank you.

Jesus had just miraculously healed these ten men. You'd think they would have been bursting with happy gratitude. Yet only one of them turned back to Jesus to actually thank and worship Him. In whatever ways God blesses us, we should always want to be like the one man who came back to praise and thank God and not like the other nine!

FATHER GOD, PLEASE HELP ME NOT TO FORGET TO BE GRATEFUL. YOU ARE SO GOOD TO ME, AND I HAVE MANY BLESSINGS TO FOCUS ON. I WANT TO WORSHIP AND PRAISE AND THANK YOU FOR EVERYTHING. AMEN.

FOCUS ON THE ENDURANCE GOD GIVES

We are hard pressed on every side, but not crushed; perplexed, but not in despair; persecuted, but not abandoned; struck down, but not destroyed. We always carry around in our body the death of Jesus, so that the life of Jesus may also be revealed in our body.

2 CORINTHIANS 4:8–10 NIV

Sometimes troubles seem to come at us from every angle, as this scripture describes. When that happens, it's nearly impossible not to be consumed with worry about them and to feel defeated. But God will always help us have just enough new strength and energy not to give up. He will help us endure. He will hold us up and keep us going. He is working out His perfect plans through it all.

We can think back to times in the past when we had no idea how to get through a horrible situation, but somehow God pulled us through and we made it to the other side. He will keep on pulling us through tough situations both now and in the future—we will never be crushed or in despair or abandoned or destroyed—until one day we are in His presence forever.

FATHER GOD, I TRUST THAT YOU KEEP GIVING ME MORE STRENGTH AND ENERGY AND ENDURANCE EXACTLY WHEN I FEEL LIKE GIVING UP. I WILL NEVER BE DEFEATED WHEN YOU ARE HELPING ME! AMEN.

FOCUS ON THE BOOK OF HEBREWS

God, for whom and through whom everything was made, chose to bring many children into glory. And it was only right that he should make Jesus, through his suffering, a perfect leader, fit to bring them into their salvation. So now Jesus and the ones he makes holy have the same Father. That is why Jesus is not ashamed to call them his brothers and sisters.

HEBREWS 2:10–11 NLT

When our overactive minds need worthwhile things to think about, we can focus on learning more from the book of Hebrews. The writer of Hebrews (and no one seems to be sure who that writer was) wanted to teach the Jewish people who had become Christians not to go back to the customs they had practiced before Jesus came. Its main point is that Jesus is above and beyond any kind of religious ritual or sacrifice. His new covenant supersedes the old covenant.

Jesus paid for sin once for all when He died on the cross and then rose again. We can't make ourselves holy through any kind of religious practice, but we can let Jesus make us holy by accepting Him as the one true Savior who died for our sins.

FATHER, THANK YOU FOR EACH BOOK IN THE BIBLE. HELP ME AS I LEARN FROM HEBREWS AND KEEP COMING BACK TO IT IN THE FUTURE. TEACH ME HOW TO APPLY ITS TRUTH TO MY LIFE AND TO SHARE IT WITH OTHERS. PLEASE DRAW ME CLOSER TO YOU THROUGH YOUR WORD. AMEN.

BE TRULY HUMBLE

A man's pride will bring him down, but he whose spirit is without pride will receive honor.
PROVERBS 29:23 NLV

Pride gets us into a lot of trouble and causes a lot of our stress and anxiety and overthinking. Proverbs 16:18 (NLV) says, "Pride comes before being destroyed and a proud spirit comes before a fall." We should want to be humble, not prideful. That means admitting our sins and mistakes. It means not thinking of ourselves as better than other people. It means being teachable, knowing we can always keep learning from others and never trying to be a know-it-all. It doesn't mean we can't have any confidence or be happy with our accomplishments; but as humble Christians, we'll place our confidence in God's work within us, recognizing that He alone gives us the ability to accomplish good things!

FATHER GOD, I ALWAYS WANT TO BE ABLE TO ADMIT MY SIN AND MISTAKES AND BE TEACHABLE. I WANT TO GIVE YOU CREDIT AND PRAISE FOR EVERYTHING. I WANT TO BE PROUD ONLY OF YOUR GREAT WORKS. I WANT TO BE TRULY HUMBLE IN A WORLD THAT IS FULL OF SELF-PRIDE. PLEASE HELP ME WITH THIS ALL MY LIFE. AMEN.

PRAY FOR YOUR CHURCH

Those who believed what Peter said were baptized and added to the church that day—about 3,000 in all. All the believers devoted themselves to the apostles' teaching, and to fellowship, and to sharing in meals (including the Lord's Supper), and to prayer.

ACTS 2:41–42 NLT

Some churches are full of people who like to criticize every little thing. Hopefully, we never fall into being petty that way. And hopefully, we spend more time praying for our own churches and other churches than we spend overthinking everything about church. We need to be praying regularly for all churches to be strong in faithfully teaching God's whole Word in context, in shepherding people well, in glorifying God, and in watching out for false teachers who lead people astray.

Every time we walk in the doors of our churches, we can pray for the well-being and protection of the people who come. We can pray for the pastor and leaders and teachers and employees and volunteers. We can pray for our leaders to preach and follow God's Word and glorify Him in everything. We can pray that God brings more and more people to our churches to hear His truth and experience His love.

FATHER GOD, I PRAY FOR MY CHURCH TO BE PLEASING TO YOU! I PRAY FOR ALL WHO ARE A PART OF MY CHURCH AND ALL THOSE WHO NEED TO COME TO MY CHURCH TO LEARN MORE ABOUT YOU. AND I PRAY THAT YOU HELP ME TO SERVE AND BE ACTIVE IN MY CHURCH ALL MY LIFE. AMEN.

FOCUS ON THE BOOK OF JAMES

But don't just listen to God's word. You must do what it says. Otherwise, you are only fooling yourselves. For if you listen to the word and don't obey, it is like glancing at your face in a mirror. You see yourself, walk away, and forget what you look like. But if you look carefully into the perfect law that sets you free, and if you do what it says and don't forget what you heard, then God will bless you for doing it.

JAMES 1:22–25 NLT

When our overactive minds need worthwhile things to think about, we can focus on learning more from the book of James. The writer of this letter was the brother of Jesus and a leader of the church in Jerusalem. If you understand the saying "Actions speak louder than words," then you know the main point James wanted to make.

We Christians shouldn't just say we have faith. Our lives should show it by what we do. That never means our good deeds are what save us from sin. It just means that when we let Jesus save us and we have the Holy Spirit living in us, we shouldn't simply want to listen to the Word of God; we should also want to *do* what it says.

FATHER, THANK YOU FOR EACH BOOK IN THE BIBLE. HELP ME AS I LEARN FROM JAMES AND KEEP COMING BACK TO IT IN THE FUTURE. TEACH ME HOW TO APPLY ITS TRUTH TO MY LIFE AND TO SHARE IT WITH OTHERS. PLEASE DRAW ME CLOSER TO YOU THROUGH YOUR WORD. AMEN.

WHO CAN EVER BE AGAINST US?

What then shall we say to these things? If God is for us, who can be against us? He who did not spare his own Son but gave him up for us all, how will he not also with him graciously give us all things?

ROMANS 8:31–32 ESV

When we accept Jesus as Savior and are following Him, God is *with* us and *for* us. And like Romans says, if God is for us, who can possibly be against us? We have nothing to be afraid of or worried about—no situation or difficult relationship or illness or injury can ever be greater than God working in us and helping us. We need to preach that truth to our restless thoughts. And we only have to call on God in prayer and believe in His love and ability to help.

We should make it a regular part of our prayer time to praise God and tell Him how great He is. That reminds us of what awesome power we have helping us in everything we do.

YOU ARE SO GREAT AND AWESOME AND POWERFUL, GOD! YOU ARE GOOD AND STRONG AND ABLE TO DO ANYTHING! YOU ARE LOVING AND KIND AND GENEROUS! YOU ARE MY EVERYTHING, AND I PRAISE YOU! AMEN.

WHATEVER YOU DO

Let the peace of Christ rule in your hearts, to which indeed you were called in one body. And be thankful. Let the word of Christ dwell in you richly, teaching and admonishing one another in all wisdom, singing psalms and hymns and spiritual songs, with thankfulness in your hearts to God. And whatever you do, in word or deed, do everything in the name of the Lord Jesus, giving thanks to God the Father through him.

COLOSSIANS 3:15–17 ESV

Everything we put into our minds through our eyes and ears affects us. This scripture in Colossians 3 helps guide us. If we let all the teachings of Jesus and His words dwell in us richly—meaning we focus on, listen to, and obey them most of all as we try our best to live like Jesus did—we will have lives that are rich and full of wisdom. So even as we do things as simple as choosing our favorite music, we can ask ourselves, *Does this help me to focus on God and following Jesus? If not, what could I choose instead that would help me focus on Him?*

FATHER GOD, PLEASE HELP ME TO MAKE EVEN THE SMALLEST CHOICES IN MY LIFE BY THINKING ABOUT HOW THEY AFFECT MY RELATIONSHIP WITH YOU. I WANT YOUR PEACE TO RULE IN MY HEART AND YOUR WORD TO DWELL IN MY HEART RICHLY. AMEN.

FOCUS ON THE BOOKS OF 1 AND 2 PETER

You are being kept by the power of God because you put your trust in Him and you will be saved from the punishment of sin at the end of the world.

1 PETER 1:5 NLV

When our overactive minds need worthwhile things to think about, we can focus on learning more from the books of 1 and 2 Peter. Peter wrote 1 Peter to Christians all over the Roman Empire who were suffering in awful ways for following Jesus. He wanted to encourage believers and teach them that suffering could be considered a good thing. That may sound odd, but he said, "Instead, be very glad—for these trials make you partners with Christ in his suffering, so that you will have the wonderful joy of seeing his glory when it is revealed to all the world. If you are insulted because you bear the name of Christ, you will be blessed, for the glorious Spirit of God rests upon you" (1 Peter 4:13–14 NLT). And in 2 Peter, written about three years after 1 Peter, Peter encouraged Christians to keep growing in faith and warned them not to listen to false teachers.

....

....

....

....

....

....

....

....

FATHER, THANK YOU FOR EACH BOOK IN THE BIBLE. HELP ME AS I LEARN FROM 1 AND 2 PETER AND KEEP COMING BACK TO THEM IN THE FUTURE. TEACH ME HOW TO APPLY THEIR TRUTH TO MY LIFE AND TO SHARE IT WITH OTHERS. PLEASE DRAW ME CLOSER TO YOU THROUGH YOUR WORD. AMEN.

WITH CONFIDENCE

Since then we have a great high priest who has passed through the heavens, Jesus, the Son of God, let us hold fast our confession. For we do not have a high priest who is unable to sympathize with our weaknesses, but one who in every respect has been tempted as we are, yet without sin. Let us then with confidence draw near to the throne of grace, that we may receive mercy and find grace to help in time of need.

HEBREWS 4:14–16 ESV

We overthinkers sometimes have things that make us feel nervous and "less than" in this world, but because of Jesus Christ, we never have to feel intimidated about going to the royal throne of our almighty God! The Bible says we can go with complete trust and ask for His help whenever we need it, and we will receive His mercy and grace.

Knowing that truth, we never need to feel intimidated about anything. God is with us and is helping us, no matter what we face! The King of all kings encourages us to approach Him and tell our needs to Him—and that is an incredible blessing.

FATHER GOD, THANK YOU THAT I CAN COME TO YOU CONFIDENTLY. YOU INVITE AND ENCOURAGE ME TO ASK YOU FOR HELP WITH ANYTHING AND EVERYTHING. NEVER LET ME FORGET WHAT A PRECIOUS GIFT THAT IS! AMEN.

RENEW YOUR MIND

For though we live in the world, we do not wage war as the world does. The weapons we fight with are not the weapons of the world. On the contrary, they have divine power to demolish strongholds. We demolish arguments and every pretension that sets itself up against the knowledge of God, and we take captive every thought to make it obedient to Christ.

2 CORINTHIANS 10:3–5 NIV

Because we live in a world full of unbelievers, sometimes we spend too much time studying what they do and say and think—especially through entertainment and social media—and soon that seems to be all that's filling our minds. We even start to copy them and go along with trends that go against God's Word. If that's happening, we need a renewal of our minds, and God is the one to renew them! His Word says, "Do not act like the sinful people of the world. Let God change your life. First of all, let Him give you a new mind. Then you will know what God wants you to do. And the things you do will be good and pleasing and perfect" (Romans 12:2 NLV).

FATHER GOD, WHEN MY MIND IS FILLING UP WITH THE THINGS OF THIS WORLD, PLEASE RENEW MY MIND. REFOCUS IT ON YOU AND WHAT YOU WANT FOR MY LIFE! AMEN.

FOCUS ON THE BOOKS OF 1, 2, AND 3 JOHN

How happy I was to meet some of your children and find them living according to the truth, just as the Father commanded. I am writing to remind you, dear friends, that we should love one another. This is not a new commandment, but one we have had from the beginning. Love means doing what God has commanded us, and he has commanded us to love one another, just as you heard from the beginning.

2 JOHN 4–6 NLT

When our overactive minds need worthwhile things to think about, we can focus on learning more from the books of 1, 2, and 3 John, written by the apostle John, one of Jesus' original twelve disciples. When writing 1 John, John wanted to make sure the Christians then and now knew that Jesus was truly a real man, that He was also truly God, and that He dearly loves us. Since John knew Jesus so personally, as one of His closest disciples, we can trust him. The second letter is a very short one to warn against false teachers. And 3 John is another short letter to John's friend Gaius to encourage him to always do what is good and not what is evil.

FATHER, THANK YOU FOR EACH BOOK IN THE BIBLE. HELP ME AS I LEARN FROM 1, 2, AND 3 JOHN AND KEEP COMING BACK TO THEM IN THE FUTURE. TEACH ME HOW TO APPLY THEIR TRUTH TO MY LIFE AND TO SHARE IT WITH OTHERS. PLEASE DRAW ME CLOSER TO YOU THROUGH YOUR WORD. AMEN.

HE ROSE AND REBUKED THE WINDS AND THE SEA

And when [Jesus] got into the boat, his disciples followed him. And behold, there arose a great storm on the sea, so that the boat was being swamped by the waves; but he was asleep. And they went and woke him, saying, "Save us, Lord; we are perishing." And he said to them, "Why are you afraid, O you of little faith?" Then he rose and rebuked the winds and the sea, and there was a great calm. And the men marveled, saying, "What sort of man is this, that even winds and sea obey him?"

MATTHEW 8:23–27 ESV

It's not just children who feel afraid of storms sometimes. No matter our age, storms and natural disasters can be scary and stressful and fill us with anxious thoughts and fears. But in any storm, flood, hurricane, earthquake, tornado, or the like, Jesus has total power to protect. He can stop any natural disaster with just His words if He chooses to, so of course He can keep us safe.

DEAR JESUS, YOU ARE SO POWERFUL TO BE ABLE JUST TO SPEAK AND STOP THE WINDS AND THE WAVES IMMEDIATELY. HELP ME TO HAVE GREAT FAITH IN YOU AND NEVER BE AFRAID! AMEN.

STOP GRUMBLING AND COMPLAINING

Be glad you can do the things you should be doing. Do all things without arguing and talking about how you wish you did not have to do them.

PHILIPPIANS 2:14 NLV

Sometimes we overthink and stress by complaining about all the things we need to do or the tasks we don't like rather than just getting busy getting them done. We all struggle in this way because it's so easy to grumble instead of working hard with a good attitude. But God's Word says not to complain about anything! And choosing to have a bad attitude while we work just makes the job worse (and might even make it take longer).

We need to be intentional about not complaining the next time we have an unpleasant job to do. We can choose praise and prayer instead. We can ask God to help us make a habit of pushing negativity and complaints out of our minds.

FATHER GOD, HELP ME NOT TO ADD MORE STRESS TO MY LIFE WITH GRUMBLING AND NEGATIVITY. I NEED YOUR HELP ALL THE TIME TO REPLACE COMPLAINING WITH GOOD AND POSITIVE THOUGHTS, ESPECIALLY PRAISE AND WORSHIP OF YOU! AMEN.

FOCUS ON THE BOOK OF JUDE

I find that I must write about something else, urging you to defend the faith that God has entrusted once for all time to his holy people. I say this because some ungodly people have wormed their way into your churches, saying that God's marvelous grace allows us to live immoral lives. The condemnation of such people was recorded long ago, for they have denied our only Master and Lord, Jesus Christ.

JUDE 3–4 NLT

When our overactive minds need worthwhile things to think about, we can focus on learning more from the book of Jude. There must have been a lot of false teachers in ancient times, because Jude is another letter written to Jewish Christians mostly to warn them not to listen to false teaching from those who try to cover up their sin. God knew that we would need this warning again in the future too—and again and again and again—because sadly, there are all kinds of people who want to spread false teaching and try to hide their sin. We should pray earnestly for wisdom to choose right from wrong and to recognize false teachers and concealed sin.

FATHER, THANK YOU FOR EACH BOOK IN THE BIBLE. HELP ME AS I LEARN FROM JUDE AND KEEP COMING BACK TO IT IN THE FUTURE. TEACH ME HOW TO APPLY ITS TRUTH TO MY LIFE AND TO SHARE IT WITH OTHERS. PLEASE DRAW ME CLOSER TO YOU THROUGH YOUR WORD. AMEN.

GOD KEEPS TRACK OF OUR SORROWS

You keep track of all my sorrows. You have collected all my tears in your bottle.

Psalm 56:8 NLT

Sometimes we feel like we just can't help overthinking our sorrows—because unfortunately, there are so many sorrows in this world. God never meant for our world to be full of sadness and sickness and death and pain, but when sin entered the world, so did all those awful things. Through each experience that makes us cry, we must always believe how much God cares. He promises in His Word that He is near when we are brokenhearted. He heals us (Psalm 34:18; 147:3); He knows and cares about every single one of our sad tears (Psalm 56:8); and for all who believe in Jesus, He is preparing heaven, where "he will wipe every tear from [our] eyes, and there will be no more death or sorrow or crying or pain. All these things are gone forever" (Revelation 21:4 NLT).

When we're hurting, we can pray to God and cry to Him. We can let Him collect our tears, and we can focus on the truth of these scriptures. Our loving heavenly Father will help us to keep going and to find joy, and one day He will make everything right.

FATHER GOD, THANK YOU FOR CARING ABOUT EVERY TEAR I CRY. I TRUST YOU AND WANT TO FOLLOW YOU, NO MATTER WHAT SORROWS I EXPERIENCE. MY HOPE AND JOY ARE IN YOU. AMEN.

BEAUTY FROM YOUR INNER SELF

Your beauty should not come from outward adornment, such as elaborate hairstyles and the wearing of gold jewelry or fine clothes. Rather, it should be that of your inner self, the unfading beauty of a gentle and quiet spirit, which is of great worth in God's sight.

1 PETER 3:3–4 NIV

One of the silliest things to overthink is our outer appearance and constantly trying to measure up to the latest beauty and fashion trends. Of course, we should all want to do our best to present ourselves nicely. But we need to keep our outward appearance in perspective. Does real beauty and a person's value come from outer appearance? Of course not. We all know people who follow the fashion and beauty trends who have horrible character. And we all know people who never follow fashion and beauty trends, but they have kindness and love for God and others overflowing from them. God focuses on the hearts of people, not outward appearance, and we can too—for both ourselves and others.

FATHER GOD, I WANT TO BE KNOWN FOR REAL AND LASTING BEAUTY THAT COMES FROM MY HEART BECAUSE I TRULY LOVE YOU AND LOVE OTHERS. PLEASE HELP ME NOT TO THINK TOO MUCH ABOUT OUTWARD APPEARANCES—FOR MYSELF AND OTHERS TOO. AMEN.

FOCUS ON THE BOOK OF REVELATION

This is a revelation from Jesus Christ, which God gave him to show his servants the events that must soon take place. He sent an angel to present this revelation to his servant John, who faithfully reported everything he saw. This is his report of the word of God and the testimony of Jesus Christ. God blesses the one who reads the words of this prophecy to the church, and he blesses all who listen to its message and obey what it says, for the time is near.

REVELATION 1:1–3 NLT

When our overactive minds need worthwhile things to think about, we can focus on learning more from the book of Revelation. God sent an angel to John, one of Jesus' original twelve disciples, to give him visions to record. These visions were full of prophecy, imagery, and symbols of what will happen in the last days of this world. And all of that can often seem very confusing and scary. But the main point of Revelation is that Jesus is coming soon to gather those of us who love and trust in Him to take us to a new home to live peacefully and perfectly forever.

FATHER, THANK YOU FOR EACH BOOK IN THE BIBLE. HELP ME AS I LEARN FROM REVELATION AND KEEP COMING BACK TO IT IN THE FUTURE. TEACH ME HOW TO APPLY ITS TRUTH TO MY LIFE AND TO SHARE IT WITH OTHERS. PLEASE DRAW ME CLOSER TO YOU THROUGH YOUR WORD. AMEN.

WORSHIP OVER WORRIES

Oh come, let us sing to the LORD; let us make a joyful noise to the rock of our salvation! Let us come into his presence with thanksgiving; let us make a joyful noise to him with songs of praise! For the LORD is a great God, and a great King above all gods. In his hand are the depths of the earth; the heights of the mountains are his also. The sea is his, for he made it, and his hands formed the dry land. Oh come, let us worship and bow down; let us kneel before the LORD, our Maker! For he is our God, and we are the people of his pasture, and the sheep of his hand.

PSALM 95:1–7 ESV

We can cover our worries with worship songs. Great songs with lyrics that praise God and share biblical truth put our minds exactly where they need to be. Worship songs are so easy to memorize; and whether we're in a place where we can crank up the music or we need to silently sing in our heads, no one can ever stop us from worshipping God anytime or anyplace!

FATHER GOD, I WANT SONGS OF PRAISE TO YOU TO FILL MY MIND ALL THE TIME AND PUSH OUT ALL ANXIOUS THOUGHTS AND WORRIES! AMEN.

FOCUS ON HEROES OF THE FAITH

Faith shows the reality of what we hope for; it is the evidence of things we cannot see. Through their faith, the people in days of old earned a good reputation.

HEBREWS 11:1–2 NLT

We can gain much encouragement from focusing our minds on the lives of people with great faith who have gone before us. Hebrews 11 is a wonderful chapter of the Bible to help us remember a whole list of faith heroes, people like Noah and Moses and Joseph and Sarah and Rahab, who continued to believe in God and His promises even during the most difficult times. Like them, we should want to hold on to our faith no matter what. We should also think about our family members and friends who have extraordinary faith in God, those who are still living and those who have passed away. Just like the heroes of the faith in the Bible, we can continually look up to and honor them and their example.

FATHER GOD, WHEN I'M FEELING STRESSED AND WORRIED, PLEASE HELP ME TO BE ENCOURAGED BY EVERYONE WHO HAS GONE BEFORE ME WHO KEPT GREAT FAITH IN YOU NO MATTER WHAT. THANK YOU FOR THEIR EXAMPLES. PLEASE HELP ME TO IMITATE THEM. AMEN.

PRAISE GOD FOR HIS AMAZING CREATION

"Our Lord and our God, it is right for You to have the shining-greatness and the honor and the power. You made all things. They were made and have life because You wanted it that way."

REVELATION 4:11 NLV

Sometimes we must get away and give our busy minds a break. Think of your favorite city or amusement park. What God made people capable of designing and building for others to enjoy is pretty amazing. None of it compares with the beauty and awesomeness of His creation, though! Only God can create awesome natural wonders, and sometimes we need to visit them, take a hike or a paddle through them, and just enjoy them—and be in total awe of His artistry and His power in creation. We can pray to God with gratitude and praise for the beauty and majesty of nature all around us. As we do so, we can let God fill us with His powerful peace.

FATHER GOD, YOU ARE SO AWESOME TO HAVE CREATED SUCH A BEAUTIFUL WORLD FOR US TO LIVE AND GROW IN. DRAW ME CLOSER TO YOU AS I FOCUS ON AND APPRECIATE EVERYTHING YOU HAVE MADE. AMEN.

FOCUS ON PEACE FROM THE SHEPHERD

The Lord is my shepherd, I lack nothing.

Psalm 23:1 NIV

Sometimes we need to let our tired, busy minds focus on the comfort and peace of well-known Psalm 23 as we pray. God is our loving shepherd, but if we're not following Him, where will we end up? But if we do let Him lead and protect us, we'll find everything we need—plus peace and joy in any situation.

Psalm 23 continues:

> *He makes me lie down in green pastures, he leads me beside quiet waters, he refreshes my soul. He guides me along the right paths for his name's sake. Even though I walk through the darkest valley, I will fear no evil, for you are with me; your rod and your staff, they comfort me. You prepare a table before me in the presence of my enemies. You anoint my head with oil; my cup overflows. Surely your goodness and love will follow me all the days of my life, and I will dwell in the house of the Lord forever. (Psalm 23:2–6 NIV)*

DEAR LORD, THANK YOU FOR BEING MY SHEPHERD AND PROVIDING EVERYTHING I NEED. YOU CALM ALL MY FEARS AND WORRIES, AND YOU FILL ME WITH YOUR PEACE AS YOU LEAD AND GUIDE ME. AMEN.

WAIT FOR THE LORD AND PRAY

Wait for the Lord; be strong and take heart and wait for the Lord.

Psalm 27:14 NIV

Sometimes when we're waiting on a big change in life or help for a big decision, it seems like nothing is happening. But God might be doing major work behind the scenes that we have no idea about. So we need to turn our wait times into more prayer time. We can ask God to show us His plans and His purposes, and then wait patiently. We might be amazed at what He lets us see! And even when His answer is "Keep waiting," we can pray for more trust in Him even when we can't see what He's doing.

Our heavenly Father is always working for our good, whether we understand wait times or not. And we can always praise Him with gratitude for simply being His children.

FATHER GOD, MY BUSY BRAIN WANTS TO KNOW ALL THE DETAILS, SO IT'S HARD TO WAIT AND NOT KNOW EXACTLY HOW YOU MIGHT BE WORKING BEHIND THE SCENES. BUT I TRUST YOU AND LOVE YOU, AND I'M SO THANKFUL I'M YOURS. AMEN.

HOW LONG?

I wait for the LORD, my whole being waits, and in his word I put my hope.
I wait for the Lord more than watchmen wait for the morning.
PSALM 130:5–6 NIV

When we feel like God is taking way too long to answer our prayers, we can find comfort and peace in the fact that the prophet Habakkuk felt impatient too. He prayed, "O Lord, how long must I call for help before You will hear? I cry out to You, 'We are being hurt!' But You do not save us" (Habakkuk 1:2 NLV).

And we can learn from God's response that our human minds can never fully know and understand what God is doing when it feels like He's taking much too long to answer our prayers: "Look among the nations, and see! Be surprised and full of wonder! For I am doing something in your days that you would not believe if you were told" (Habakkuk 1:5 NLV).

FATHER GOD, PLEASE HELP ME TO REMEMBER THAT JUST BECAUSE I FEEL IMPATIENT, THAT DOESN'T MEAN YOU ARE NOT WORKING OUT YOUR PLANS IN EXACTLY THE RIGHT WAYS—WAYS I CAN'T EVEN COMPREHEND. YOU ARE GOOD, AND I TRUST YOU AND HOPE IN YOU. AMEN.

BE STILL AND FOCUS ON GOD

"Be still, and know that I am God."

Psalm 46:10 esv

Our smartphones are fantastic with all the things they can do and ways they can help us stay in touch and informed. On the other hand, they can also be extremely distracting and a huge source of stress and anxiety. They can take our thoughts away from what we need to be thinking about, and the worst is when our thoughts can't focus on God.

God knows and understands that we have distractions in this life, but we need to work hard to put them out of our minds when we pray and study His Word, remembering who it is we're talking to and learning from—the King of kings! We should go to God with our full attention on Him, with respect and total devotion, with humble and sincere gratitude that He lets us come to Him at any time—that's amazing!

FATHER GOD, HELP ME TO BE STILL AND RESPECTFUL BEFORE YOU, WITH MY THOUGHTS AND CONVERSATION TOTALLY FOCUSED ON YOU AND DEVOTED TO YOU! AMEN.

BE STILL AND PRAY

Trust in the L*ORD, and do good; dwell in the land and befriend faithfulness. Delight yourself in the* L*ORD, and he will give you the desires of your heart. Commit your way to the* L*ORD; trust in him, and he will act. He will bring forth your righteousness as the light, and your justice as the noonday. Be still before the* L*ORD and wait patiently for him; fret not yourself over the one who prospers in his way, over the man who carries out evil devices!*

PSALM 37:3–7 ESV

When we pray, we need to be still like scripture says. We should be patient without fretting, steadying our minds and hearts to concentrate on who God is and how much praise He deserves. We should praise Him and tell Him of our love for Him. We should ask for forgiveness for our sins and thank Him for being our Savior. And we should tell Him all of our needs and our loved ones' needs. He loves to hear from us and help us, with endless mercy and grace.

DEAR LORD, YOU ARE KING OF KINGS AND ALMIGHTY CREATOR. YOU ARE MY SAVIOR FROM SIN. YOU ARE ALL THIS AND MORE, AND YOU ARE MY LOVING HEAVENLY FATHER AS WELL. I AM BEYOND BLESSED TO BE ABLE TO COME TO YOU IN PRAYER. YOU KNOW MY THOUGHTS AND NEEDS AND WORRIES, AND YOU CARE ABOUT EACH ONE. I BRING THEM TO YOU TODAY, AND I ASK FOR YOUR HELP AND YOUR PEACE. AMEN.

AVOID DRAMA

"Blessed are the peacemakers, for they will be called children of God."
MATTHEW 5:9 NIV

The world has plenty of stress, so we surely don't need to add any extra unnecessarily. Yet we all know that some people seem to love drama just for the sake of drama. If some kind of drama isn't happening, they'll create it. We shouldn't love being in conflict and competition with others; instead, we should always want good and peaceful relationships, forgiving one another and not gossiping or causing fights.

Yet the Bible says blessed are the peace*makers*, and you can't *make* anything without some work involved. So making peace takes working out of disagreements and trouble, not just going along with everything to try to keep everyone happy and drama-free. We need help and wisdom from God to know how to do this right. Fortunately, God promises us that He loves to give us wisdom (see James 1:5). He loves to help us with our problems, so we should keep on asking!

FATHER GOD, HELP ME TO AVOID DRAMA YET ALSO BE WILLING TO WORK OUT CONFLICT AND BE A PEACEMAKER. I AM GRATEFUL FOR YOUR WISDOM AND HELP. I NEED YOU SO MUCH! AMEN.

LOOK FORWARD

I forget everything that is behind me and look forward to that which is ahead of me. My eyes are on the crown. I want to win the race and get the crown of God's call from heaven through Christ Jesus. All of us who are full-grown Christians should think this way. If you do not think this way, God will show it to you. So let us keep on obeying the same truth we have already been following.

PHILIPPIANS 3:13–16 NLV

We often have a hard time letting go, and we overthink and worry too much about giving things up and experiencing change. When it's time for something new in our lives, we want to cling to the old. Or sometimes we don't want to share what we have with others because we're afraid that once we do then we won't have enough.

But we can't accept new gifts from God if we keep a tight fist clutching what we already have. Open hands that are willing to let go when we need to are hands that can receive new gifts.

....

....

....

....

....

....

....

....

FATHER GOD, PLEASE HELP ME TO REMEMBER THAT EVERY GOOD THING IS A BLESSING FROM YOU, AND HELP ME TO UNCLENCH MY GRIP FROM THE GIFTS YOU GIVE ME. HELP ME TO KNOW WHEN I NEED TO LET GO AND BE GENEROUS AND WILLING TO EXPERIENCE THE NEW THINGS YOU ARE DOING IN MY LIFE AND THE NEW GIFTS YOU ARE GIVING. AMEN.

ALL OF A SUDDEN

Be strong in the Lord and in the strength of his might.

EPHESIANS 6:10 ESV

Sometimes we are unexpectedly thrown into something new with no time to prepare. That's both good and bad. On the one hand, it's stressful; and on the other, it means we won't have time to overthink it beforehand—we'll just have to jump in the deep end and start swimming. Can you think of a time when something like that has happened to you?

Sometimes God lets that happen on purpose so we can get over our fears and worries and so He can show us how we can depend on Him most of all for His help. He is always there, and we can always call on Him in prayer. We might be surprised at what we are capable of, even with no prep time beforehand, with His power working in us!

FATHER GOD, SOMETIMES I SUDDENLY FIND MYSELF IN A SITUATION WHERE I DON'T HAVE A CLUE WHAT TO DO BECAUSE I DIDN'T PLAN AND PREPARE! HELP ME TO REALIZE HOW MUCH I CAN DEPEND ON YOU AND YOUR POWER IN THOSE TIMES. TEACH ME WHAT YOU WANT ME TO LEARN IN MY UNEXPECTED, UNPLANNED CIRCUMSTANCES, AND STRENGTHEN MY FAITH IN YOU, PLEASE! AMEN.

ENDURANCE, CHARACTER, AND HOPE

We can rejoice, too, when we run into problems and trials, for we know that they help us develop endurance. And endurance develops strength of character, and character strengthens our confident hope of salvation. And this hope will not lead to disappointment. For we know how dearly God loves us, because he has given us the Holy Spirit to fill our hearts with his love.

ROMANS 5:3–5 NLT

It's easy to despise and feel defeated by the problems and troubles we face that cause us to overthink. But we need to remember that when we depend on Jesus to help us get through them, those trials are also doing good things for us—they are helping us develop endurance. And like Romans 5:3–5 says, that helps us develop strong character, which then strengthens our confident hope of salvation in Jesus!

God's Word promises that our hope in Him will never disappoint us. So as hard as trials are, we can't forget about the good things they can do for us as well. We can stick close to Jesus in prayer and time in God's Word and let Him love and lead us.

FATHER GOD, PLEASE HELP ME TO REJOICE IN MY TRIALS BECAUSE OF THE GOOD WORK YOU'RE DOING IN ME THROUGH THEM. REJOICING IN TRIALS IS HARD, BUT YOU WANT ME TO LEARN TO DEPEND ON YOU THROUGH THEM, AND THAT KIND OF DEPENDENCE IS SUCH A BLESSING! THANK YOU FOR LOVING ME SO WELL. AMEN.

CLOSE TO GOD

Come close to God and He will come close to you. Wash your hands, you sinners. Clean up your hearts, you who want to follow the sinful ways of the world and God at the same time. Be sorry for your sins and cry because of them. Be sad and do not laugh. Let your joy be turned to sorrow. Let yourself be brought low before the Lord. Then He will lift you up and help you.

JAMES 4:8–10 NLV

Sometimes when we're overthinking and worrying and trying to pray, God feels far away. But we have to ask ourselves, *Whose fault is that? Does it have anything to do with what my relationship with God has looked like lately?*

Each one of us must put intentional time and effort into our relationship with Jesus. He is the Savior of everyone who believes in Him, but He doesn't want to be a distant Savior we meet once and never hang out with again. He wants to be our closest friend, and He is constantly with us through His Holy Spirit! We grow closer to Jesus by regularly spending time reading the Bible, going to a Bible-teaching church, serving others in Jesus' name, and praying to Him all the time.

DEAR JESUS, I WANT YOU AS MY TRUE CLOSE FRIEND. I WANT A STRONG AND STEADY RELATIONSHIP WITH YOU. WHEN I WANDER FAR FROM YOU, PLEASE HELP ME COME NEAR TO YOU AGAIN. THANK YOU FOR ALWAYS BEING THERE FOR ME! AMEN.

SERVE!

"'For I was hungry and you gave Me food to eat. I was thirsty and you gave Me water to drink. . . .' Then those that are right with God will say, 'Lord, when did we see You hungry and feed You? When did we see You thirsty and give You a drink? . . .' Then the King will say, 'For sure, I tell you, because you did it to one of the least of My brothers, you have done it to Me.'"

MATTHEW 25:35, 37, 40 NLV

We overthinkers need to stay close to Jesus by reading God's Word daily, praying continually, worshipping God, and learning at church. And the above scripture shows us how to be extra close to Jesus. We serve Him directly when we feed the hungry, give water to the thirsty, share clothes with the needy, and so on. And when we serve others in need, it often helps get our minds off our own worries and fills us with gratitude and joy because of our blessings.

We should pray for God to show us many opportunities for service all of our lives! There's little time for useless overthinking when we're caring more about others than ourselves.

DEAR JESUS, I WANT TO GET MY MIND OFF USELESS OVERTHINKING BY SERVING YOU AND DRAWING CLOSE TO YOU. SHOW ME WHERE, WHEN, AND HOW TO SERVE OTHERS MORE. AMEN.

SUPERPOWER OF THE HOLY SPIRIT

"But when he, the Spirit of truth, comes, he will guide you into all the truth. He will not speak on his own; he will speak only what he hears, and he will tell you what is yet to come. He will glorify me because it is from me that he will receive what he will make known to you."

John 16:13–14 NIV

Often the thing we're stressing about and overthinking is what *might* happen in the future. Wouldn't it be nice to have a superpower that enabled you to see into the future, warning you of danger and bad situations, and helping you to make choices that would always bring you blessing and never harm? In a way, all of us who have the Holy Spirit because we have committed our lives to Christ (Romans 8) actually *do* have a superpower. Pray and ask the Spirit to come alive in you today.

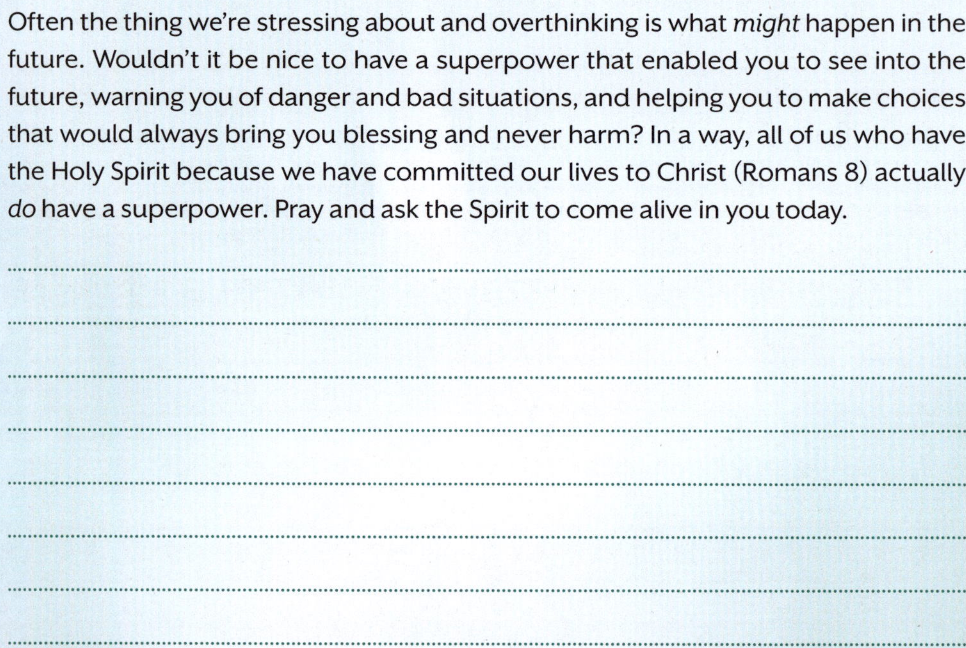

FATHER GOD, I CAN'T SEE INTO THE FUTURE, BUT I KNOW YOU CAN. I NEED YOUR HOLY SPIRIT IN ME TO WARN ME OF DANGER AND SITUATIONS THAT WOULD BE BAD FOR ME. PLEASE RAISE RED FLAGS AND CLOSE DOORS AND HELP ME SENSE YOUR DIRECTION AWAY FROM WHAT IS HARMFUL FOR ME. POINT ME TOWARD WHAT IS GOOD FOR ME, ACCORDING TO YOUR WILL. I DON'T NEED TO BE WORRIED OR AFRAID OF THE FUTURE; I SIMPLY NEED TO TRUST IN AND DEPEND ON YOU, YOUR POWER, YOUR PERFECT PLANS, AND YOUR LOVE. AMEN.

MASTERPIECE

We are God's masterpiece. He has created us anew in Christ Jesus, so we can do the good things he planned for us long ago.

EPHESIANS 2:10 NLT

Overthinking and self-doubt and cruel things people say can sometimes have us questioning our value and our purpose in this crazy world. This scripture is a good one to memorize, a great reminder to give us confidence and peace and hope.

Not one of us is an accident. Our lives have purpose and meaning that God planned when He created us.

FATHER GOD, THANK YOU FOR CREATING ME TOTALLY UNIQUE. EVEN MY FINGERPRINTS ARE UNLIKE THOSE OF ANY OTHER PERSON IN THE WORLD. I BELIEVE YOU HAVE GOOD PLANS FOR ME AND GOOD WORKS YOU WANT ME TO DO, AND I BELIEVE MY LIFE WILL BE BEST WHEN I'M FOLLOWING THOSE PLANS AND DOING THOSE WORKS! WILL YOU PLEASE SHOW AND GUIDE ME EVERY DAY? PLEASE PUT DESIRES IN MY HEART AND MIND THAT MATCH THE THINGS YOU WANT ME TO DO. PLEASE OPEN DOORS OF OPPORTUNITY YOU WANT ME TO WALK THROUGH AND CLOSE DOORS YOU DON'T WANT FOR ME. I WANT TO LIVE A LIFE OF SERVING YOU AND FOLLOWING YOUR WILL FOR ME. I BELIEVE THAT IS THE MOST REWARDING KIND OF LIFE! AMEN.

FOCUS ON THE FATHER'S WILL

[Jesus] withdrew about a stone's throw beyond them, knelt down and prayed, "Father, if you are willing, take this cup from me; yet not my will, but yours be done." An angel from heaven appeared to him and strengthened him. And being in anguish, he prayed more earnestly, and his sweat was like drops of blood falling to the ground.

LUKE 22:41–44 NIV

Jesus gave us our very best example of what to focus on when our thoughts are overwhelming us. He was consumed with anxious thoughts before His death on the cross—so consumed and so anxious that some versions of the Bible say His sweat was like drops of blood falling to the ground.

We can take heart that even while He was perfect, Jesus still stressed too. And the main focus of His prayer to the Father was "not my will, but yours be done." We too should always pray to God in whatever situation we're facing, "God, I ask You for this, but if Your answer is no, I accept that because I want Your will to be done more than my will."

FATHER GOD, I BRING BEFORE YOU THINGS I WANT OR THINK I NEED AND PLANS THAT I WANT TO WORK OUT. YET I KNOW THAT YOUR WILL AND YOUR PLANS ARE ALWAYS GREATER THAN MINE. SO I PRAY THAT YOUR WILL BE DONE IN ALL THINGS. PLEASE HELP ME TO STAY STEADFAST AND FAITHFUL IN THIS PRAYER. AMEN.

SCRIPTURE INDEX

OLD TESTAMENT

NEW TESTAMENT